*REDUCING EMPLOYEE
ABSENTEEISM
THROUGH
SELF-MANAGEMENT
TRAINING*

REDUCING EMPLOYEE ABSENTEEISM THROUGH SELF-MANAGEMENT TRAINING

A Research-Based Analysis and Guide

COLETTE A. FRAYNE

Foreword by Gary P. Latham

Q
Quorum Books
New York • Westport, Connecticut • London

Library of Congress Cataloging-in-Publication Data

Frayne, Colette A.
    Reducing employee absenteeism through self-management training : a
research-based analysis and guide / Colette A. Frayne; foreword by Gary P. Latham.
        p.   cm.
    Includes bibliographical references (p.).
    ISBN 0-89930-553-9 (lib. bdg. : alk. paper)
    1. Absenteeism (Labor)   2. Personnel management.   3. Self-
evaluation.   I. Title.
HD5115.F73   1991
331.25 '98—dc20   90-8407

British Library Cataloguing in Publication Data is available.

Library of Congress Catalog Card Number: 90-8407
ISBN: 0-89930-553-9

First published in 1991

Quorum Books, 88 Post Road West, Westport, CT   06881
An imprint of Greenwood Publishing Group, Inc.

Printed in the United States of America

The paper used in this book complies with the
Permanent Paper Standard issued by the National
Information Standards Organization (Z39.48-1984).

10 9 8 7 6 5 4 3 2 1

To my parents, John and Lucille,
and to my husband, J. Michael Geringer,
for their invincible love, support,
inspiration, and dear friendship.

CONTENTS

FIGURES AND TABLES

FIGURES

TABLES

FOREWORD

This book is an expanded and revised work based on a doctoral dissertation that I had the intellectual stimulation and sheer enjoyment of supervising in my role as chairman of the Dissertation Committee in the Graduate School of Business at the University of Washington. The dissertation was chosen as the very best in 1986 by both the Society of Industrial-Organizational Psychology of the American Psychological Association and the Division of Organizational Behavior of the Academy of Management. The awards from these two scholarly societies were in response to Dr. Frayne's groundbreaking developments in teaching employees the science of self-management. The two awards underscored the scientific rigor with which Dr. Frayne had conducted her work, as did the publication of her findings in the prestigious *Journal of Applied Psychology*.

That Dr. Frayne's work is replicable by human resource specialists who lack scientific training was shown in follow-up work. Again, the quality with which this work was carried out led to a second publication in the *Journal of Applied Psychology* and a write-up in *Proceed-ings of the Academy of Management.*

The importance of this book lies in its shift in emphasis from a scientific audience to human resource practitioners in organizational settings. Dr. Frayne explains why self-management is a critical skill for hourly employees in organizations that are striving to be cost-effective. She briefly summarizes in everyday language the hard evidence that conclusively demonstrates the effectiveness of self-management training techniques. She then describes in detail how trainers can use these techniques to teach self-management to employees, and conclusively demonstrates the correlation between the training and employee attendance. Finally, she looks into some of the wider applications of self-management training in the workplace—managerial performance, managing international joint ventures, and reduction of work-related stress. Nowhere else, to my knowledge, does this level of detail exist for the human resource training community. Dr. Frayne's insights in this book will be appreciated keenly by all of us who want to assist employees in becoming productive individuals in the workplace.

Gary P. Latham, Professor
Graduate School of Business
University of Washington

ACKNOWLEDGMENTS

I have been studying self-management for over five years now. The results of my research endeavors have evolved into the writing of this book. The book is based in part on my doctoral dissertation, which was completed at the University of Washington in Seattle, and on the subsequent research.

It is with great pride and admiration that I extend special thanks to my mentor, Dr. Gary P. Latham, for his tremendous support and invaluable guidance throughout all phases of this research endeavor. I am especially indebted to Dr. Cecil H. Bell for his sincere, continued guidance and friendship and the instrumental role that he played for me during my entire graduate training; to Dr. Thomas W. Lee, who taught me the importance of sound theory and statistical inference as well as the necessity to achieve excellence in one's research endeavors; and to Dr. Robert Woodworth, Dr. Lee Roy Beach, and Dr. Robert Crutchfield for their cooperation and commitment to serving on my supervisory committee.

I am extremely grateful to Dr. Horace D. Beach, Professor of Psychology at the University of Victoria, for his advice during the design phase of this research; to Dr. James Rosenzweig for his assistance in obtaining the organizational site for both studies; and to Victoria Pack for her friendship, enthusiasm, and assistance with all phases of the training program.

For their contributions I also wish to thank the individuals who participated as subjects in this study, their supervisors, and staff for their cooperation during the data collection phase of the study. Special heartfelt thanks to my personal friends, who supported me throughout an extremely demanding yet incredibly rewarding time during my personal life: Michelle Armor, Walt Blacconiere, Jane Clark, Kelly Foy, Jody Fry, Sandy Gillam, Phil Hunsaker, Diane Llewellyn, Terry Mitchell, Nona Pedersen, and Bill Scott.

When I decided to publish my doctoral dissertation and the follow-up work, a substantial number of revisions and additions were needed. I owe special thanks to my secretary and friend, Pat Neatby, who worked many long, hard hours to ensure that the book was prepared properly. In the same light, I owe a special thanks to the "person behind the scenes" who turned my academic jargon into easier reading and kept me going throughout all the revisions, Pam Young. I would also like to thank my production editor, Catherine A. Lyons, for her willingness to "step in" and see this book through to completion. And finally, a special gratitude to my editor, Liliane H. Miller, for her patience and willingness to "go beyond" the normal editorial duties in championing this project through to its final stages. Without these four individuals, I could not have completed this goal.

I wish to express sincere appreciation to my husband, J. Michael Geringer, for his unconditional love, unending patience, and invaluable support during the four years of sharing mutual joys and frustrations as we both pursued our doctoral educations. And most important, I am grateful to my parents and best friends, John and Lucille Frayne, who have always encouraged me to pursue my educational goals and career aspirations, to have the courage to explore my independence and my dreams, and to be proud and appreciative of the unconquerable strength and love that our family has always been fortunate to share.

1

WHY SELF-MANAGEMENT?
WHAT IS SELF-MANAGEMENT?

INTRODUCTION

As employees' demands for flexibility, autonomy, and challenge increase, managers are struggling to find an approach that accommodates both the employees' need for freedom and the organization's need for control. Self-management training may be one solution. Training individuals in self-management has reduced employee absenteeism, improved job performance, and enabled employees at all hierarchical levels to manage themselves more effectively. In addition, improvement in self-efficacy, that belief necessary to overcome personal and motivational obstacles, has allowed individuals to achieve and maintain their set goals and performance standards.

Traditionally, many firms have used excessive and frequently negative means to control their employees at all hierarchical levels in an attempt to ensure that employee behavior is consistent with the organization's goals. Needed now is a better understanding of management methods that enable people to manage themselves more effectively, both with the organization's help and on their own. In today's environment, both management and nonmanagement workers require enchanced self-management skills if they are to cope well with new pressures—such as from increased autonomy and participation— when they arise.

WHY SELF-MANAGEMENT?

Because it works. In working life, as in personal life, individuals can play the major part in managing their affairs. A successful employee manages his or her own progress. A successful manager manages his or her own team. A manager is expected to plan, set deadlines, direct and supervise others, maintain high morale and satisfaction among the employees, and achieve his or her own performance objectives.

Now, when an office or department is running smoothly—people are doing their jobs effectively, morale is high, and work is getting done on time—self-management training may seem hardly necessary. Unfortunately, however, few organizations function like this for very long. Far from it. Work becomes routine and boring. There are continual interruptions, telephone calls, unscheduled visitors. It's not surprising that anyone—manager or subordinate—trying to survive this sort of chaos soon gives up hope of even coming close to what started out as performance targets.

In the face of competing demands on time and resources, it is essential that a manager have clearly stated objectives; objectives alone, however, are not sufficient for effectively managing within an often unpredictable work environment. Self-management can provide a personalized program for improving an individual's own behavior and exercising greater control over aspects of his or her decision making.

Bandura's (Bandura, 1977a) social learning theory holds that one can consciously manipulate environment to produce the end results desired. How we behave has to do not only with what we see happening, but also with how we perceive our situation plus the long- or short-term effects of these perceptions.

This book seeks to explain, support, and suggest strategies for successful self-management in the workplace—specifically in regard to employee attendance, a chronic workplace problem with estimated annual costs of $30 billion in the United States alone (Steers & Rhodes, 1984). The book presents and discusses the findings of two studies that investigated the impact of self-management training on employee attendance. As noted elsewhere, industrial absenteeism is a chronic problem in organizations (Cruikshank, 1976; Goodman & Atkin, 1984; Hedges, 1973; Yolles, Carone, & Krinske, 1975). Employee absences disrupt work schedules, increase costs, and decrease productivity.

Yet despite the magnitude of the absenteeism problem, we know little about its causes or how to manage it (Goodman & Atkin, 1984). Methodological problems regarding the measurement of absenteeism plague both the interpretation and the evaluation of research in this area (Muchinsky, 1977). In short, absenteeism continues to be a "social fact in need of a theory" (As, 1962; Fichman, 1984).

WHAT IS SELF-MANAGEMENT?

Self-management (Mills, 1983) or self-regulation (Slocum & Sims, 1980) is an effort by an individual to control his or her behavior. Self-management (Mills, 1983) involves goal setting, establishing a contract, monitoring the ways in which the environment is hindering the attainment of the goals, and administering reinforcement or punishment based on self-evaluation. The first step in effective self-management is for the individual to set and commit to specific goals (Kanfer, 1975). Otherwise, self-monitoring—obviously a precondition for self-evaluation—has no effect on behvaior (Simon, 1979). Written contracts increase goal commitment by spelling out the reinforcing conditions for accepting the goal (Erez & Kanfer, 1983).

WHAT INFLUENCES SELF-MANAGEMENT?

Dissatisfaction. A sense of lack of progress. An inability to manage one's own behavior. Once an individual sets personal goals, the gap between goal and reality can spur that person to take active charge.

How? By self-management, an organized system for change. Self-management is a skill developed through a training program that teaches basic techniques and then measures performance over time. Self-management involves the following activities:

1. Realizing what the problem is (self-assessment)
2. Establishing goals to deal with the problem (goal setting)

3. Monitoring the situations that keep one from reaching those goals (self-monitoring)
4. Evaluating the success of the plan and refining or changing tactics if necessary (self-evaluation)

Effective self-management requires goal setting and commitment. The commitment includes two further phases—contract and maintenance. The contract is with oneself; maintenance ensures that the new behaviors continue to be used.

HOW DOES SELF-MANAGEMENT WORK?

Training in self-management leads to positive outcomes by enhancing a person's sense of self-efficacy (Bandura, 1977b, 1978b, 1982). Self-efficacy is a measure of a person's conviction that he or she can successfully perform the behavior or behaviors that a given situation requires. Such conviction influences both the acquisition of coping behavior and the effort that a person is willing to expend in order to maintain that behavior in the face of real or perceived obstacles. People who judge themselves unable to cope with environmental demands perceive their difficulties (for example, family problems, transportation) as more formidable than they are in actual fact. People with a strong sense of self-efficacy, by contrast, focus their attention and effort on the demands of the situation (for example, coming to work) and are spurred on by perceived obstacles to an increase—rather than a decrease—in effort.

Training in self-management relates directly to a person's desire and willingness to practice more self-control than previously. Self-controlling behaviors are initiated when a choice point is reached: when a person's attention is directed toward a specific behavior (for example, a supervisor announces that continued absence from work will lead to a one-day suspension), when changes in reinforcement occur (for example, a good attendance record formerly ignored by management is now noted and praised), or when expected outcomes are no longer forthcoming (for example, taking the day off from work loses some of its enjoyment). The choice point has been reached; the self-management process can begin (Kanfer & Karoly, 1972).

STAGES IN SELF-MANAGEMENT

A person who has had a major effect on the clinical practice of self-management is Kanfer. Together with Karoly, he presented a model of self-management that involves three distinct stages. First, self-observation or self-assessment gives the individual a baseline for evaluating change. On the basis of the individual's past experience and expectations as to what should happen in a given situation, he or she sets specific performance goals.

Second, the person compares the information provided by self-observation with the behavior goals. At this stage, self-monitoring begins. If the behaviors are exceeding the goal, he or she can set higher goals (Bandura, 1977a).

The third stage involves self-administration of reinforcers or punishers related to the degree to which the behavior diverges from the performance goals. Support for this model has been obtained in both laboratory settings (for example, Kanfer, 1970; Mahoney, Moura, & Wade, 1973) and clinical settings (for example, Kanfer, 1975; Kanfer et al., 1974; Karoly & Kanfer, 1982).

It is important to note that these self-management stages are inter-related. Self-monitoring and self-evaluation *without* goal setting have no lasting effect on behavior following a performance appraisal (Watson & Tharp, 1981; Erez, 1977; Locke et al, 1981; Campbell, 1982).

The contract is a crucial part of self-management training. This is a written agreement with oneself specifying expectations, plans, and contingencies for changing behavior (Epstein & Wing, 1979; Kanfer, 1980; O'Banion & Whaley, 1981). The contract specifies (1) the goal(s); (2) the actions the person will take to reach them; and (3) the contingencies for self-administering the reinforcers or punishers.

Obviously the chief test of self-management training, once it has been accomplished, is maintenance (Hall, 1980). Does the behavior change remain in effect? The answer depends largely on whether the individual has been allowed to practice the desired skills during the training program (Goldstein & Kanfer, 1979), is encouraged to practice them in different situations, and continually self-monitors his or her performance (Watson & Tharp, 1984).

HOW DOES SELF-MANAGEMENT RELATE TO ABSENTEEISM IN THE WORKPLACE?

As demonstrated in my own research (Frayne & Latham, 1987; Latham & Frayne, 1989), individuals who receive training in self-management acquire knowledge on how to overcome obstacles preventing them from coming to work, increase their self-efficacy and outcome expectancies, and thus increase their attendance on the job.

The question of how we know that self-management works is taken up in Chapters 2 and 3. Chapter 4 discusses research results as well as the significance of these findings for research and practice. Chapter 5 explains how to use self-management and what considerations should one keep in mind when adopting a self-management program. Chapter 6 touches on self-management's wider applications, as well as directions for future research.

SUMMARY

Social learning theory holds that a person can consciously manipulate his or her environment to produce the end results aimed for. Self-management training teaches skills that enable people to take active control over their affairs—goal setting, establishing a contract, self-monitoring, and administering reinforcement or punishment based on self-evaluation. Recent research suggests that self-management training can dramatically affect employee attendance in the workplace. The purpose of this book is to show the practicing manager how to use self-management training effectively.

2

EVIDENCE THAT
SELF-MANAGEMENT WORKS:
THE FOUNDATION STUDIES

INTRODUCTION

As a basis for instructing managers in the effective use of self-management training, we do well at this point to examine earlier studies and theories that were its forerunners.

In the past decade, one area of social learning theory that has been investigated empirically is behavior modeling (Goldstein & Sorcher, 1974; Latham & Saari, 1979). Behavior change can take place as a result of observing another person's behavior and its consequences. In fact, one excellent procedure for achieving lasting behavior change is induction through modeling, refinement through enactment, and reinforcement through successful practice (Bandura, 1977a).

In the past ten years, scholars (Luthans & Davis, 1979; Manz & Sims, 1980; Mills, 1983) have advocated the use of self-management techniques in organizational settings. The need to reduce levels of supervision, meet employees' demands for autonomy and challenging jobs, and establish offices in the home have aroused interest in self-management among executives in both the private and the public sectors.

Why should attendance in the workplace be affected by self-management techniques? The answer to this can be inferred from Kanfer's work with people dependent on drugs or alcohol (Erez & Kanfer, 1983; Kanfer, 1970; Kanfer & Bursemeyer, 1982; Kanfer & Karoly, 1972). Kanfer's model of self-management focuses on two important components—the sequence of goal-related events and the individual as the source of control over his or her behavior during those events.

In the area of attendance, as well, self-management involves a comparison of one's performance against the goals one has set. Plainly, many people besides those dependent on drugs or alcohol also perceive themselves as unable to overcome problems—in this case, problems interfering with their attendance at work. That is, they have low self-efficacy and are caught in a vicious circle in which the perceived inability to cope reinforces itself.

This chapter reviews behavioral and cognitive theories that were precursors to social learning theory. It examines social learning theory as a theoretical framework encompassing critical variables in both cognitive and operant psychology—expectancies, goal setting, and reinforcers. Empirical research on four primary variables in social learning theory are then reviewed—behavior modeling, self-management, self-efficacy, and outcome expectancies. The chapter concludes with an overview of the absenteeism literature.

BEHAVIORAL THEORIES

Two behavioral theories that preceded social learning theory include Hull's theory (1943) on drive reduction and Skinner's (1953) research on operant conditioning. Drive theory and operant conditioning are similar in that both theories are based in part upon Thorndike's (1911) law of effect. That is, where past actions result in positive consequences, individuals tend to repeat those actions; where past actions result in negative consequences, individuals tend not to repeat them. The two theories differ primarily in the emphasis placed on an individual's internal drives versus environmental contingencies as a means of predicting, understanding, and controlling behavior.

Drive Theory

Hull (1943) argued that behavior is motivated by primary and secondary drives. He defined "drive" as an energizing influence that determines the intensity of behavior and theoretically increases along with the level of deprivation. Whereas primary drives (e.g., hunger, thirst, sex) are biologically based, secondary drives are learned through their temporal association with the reduction of a primary drive.

Empirical research did not support Hull's (1943) crucial hypothesis that all behavior can be explained in terms of a reduction in primary drives. Olds and Milner (1954) found that an increase—rather than a reduction—in drive increased the frequency with which a behavior is repeated. When electrodes were implanted in the rat's lateral hypothalamus and electrical current run through it, the rat repeated those actions that had been immediately preceded by electrical stimulation. Electrical stimulation served as a reinforcer. In a subsequent study, Olds (1958) found that sexual intromission served as a reinforcer for rats even though they were not allowed to ejaculate.

Operant Conditioning

One of the dominant influences in American psychology is the work of B. F. Skinner (Heyduk & Fenigstein, 1984). Skinner showed how voluntary human behavior is affected by environmental events that immediately follow a given behavior. He termed environmental events that increase behavior *reinforcers*. The frequency of a response can be changed by altering the presentation of a reinforcer as well as by its scheduling.

Many studies (e.g., Komaki, Waddell, & Pearce, 1977; Latham, Mitchell, & Dossett, 1978; Nord, 1969; Saari & Latham, 1982) have demonstrated the effectiveness of behavior modification procedures in organizational setting. One of the most publicized studies was conducted at Emery Air Freight (Feeney, 1973). Performance during a baseline period was compared with performance after the introduction of reinforcement techniques. Major characteristics of the program included the measurement of performance, daily feedback, and the use of praise and recognition by supervisors as positive reinforcers. These techniques saved the company approximately $3 million over a three-year period.

One advantage of reinforcement theory is that it provides a parsimonious explanation of behavior. The theory avoids references to cognition and affect. Nevertheless, the work of Skinner and his followers has been criticized (e.g., Locke, 1977; Mitchell, 1974) on the very grounds that cognitive processes (e.g., goal setting) are needed to explain why reinforcers affect behavior. In fact, empirical research has shown that cognitive influences can weaken, distort, or nullify the effects of reinforcers (Kaufman, Baron, & Kopp, 1966).

Kaufman, Baron, and Kopp (1966) conducted a study in which one group of people was correctly informed about how often their performance would be rewarded, whereas other groups were incorrectly told that their behavior would be reinforced either every minute (fixed-interval schedule) or after they had performed 150 responses on the average (variable-ratio schedule).

The results showed that beliefs about the schedules of reinforcement outweighed the influence of what actually took place. Although everyone was rewarded on the same schedule, those who thought they were being reinforced once every minute produced a very low response rate (means = 6). Those who thought they were being reinforced on the variable-ratio schedule maintained an exceedingly high response rate (mean = 259). Those who were correctly informed that their behavior would be rewarded on the average every minute displayed an intermediate level of response. Thus identical environmental consequences can have different behavioral effects, depending on one's perceptions of them. Similar findings have been obtained by Dulany (1968) and Bandura and Barab (1971).

Today, operant methodology is considered to be a milestone in organizational psychology (Dunnette, 1976) because of the relative simplicity and specificity of its methods and the reliable outcomes that these methods produce. However, the philosophy of behaviorism, on which operant techniques are based, remains questionable.

COGNITIVE THEORIES

While drive theory and reinforcement theory attempt to explain behavior solely in terms of internal drives or environmental consequences, cognitive theories attempt to explain behavior primarily in terms of conscious mental processes. Two cognitive theories that have been investigated extensively in organizational settings are expectancy theory and goal-setting theory.

Expectancy Theory

Tolman (1932) and Lewin (1938) presented cognitively oriented theories of behavior that took into account both the person and the environment. Tolman (1932) argued that learning resulted primarily from changes in beliefs about the environment rather than from changes in the strengths of past habits. Lewin (1938, 1947) argued that past occurrences could have an effect on present behavior to the extent that they modified present environmental situations. In general, these theories were based on the idea that the strength to act in a certain way depends on the person's expectancy that the act will be followed by certain outcomes as well as on the value or attractiveness of those outcomes to the person. As a result of this earlier work, Vroom (1964) developed a theoretical framework specifically for understanding and predicting motivation in work settings, namely, expectancy theory.

Vroom's theory states that a person's choice of effort level is a function of three cognitive variables: expectancy, instrumentality, and valence. Expectancy is defined as a belief concerning the probability that an act will be followed by a particular outcome. Instrumentality refers to the perceived relationship between performance and the anticipated outcome. For example, in an organizational context, anticipated outcomes include such things as pay increases, reprimands, and recognition. Valence refers to the strength of an individual's preference for a particular outcome. An individual may have either a positive or a negative valence for an anticipated outcome (instrumentality). Vroom's formulation states that the effort an individual exerts is a function of the expectancy that certain outcomes will result from the behavior and the valence of those outcomes. Expectancy and valence are said to combine multiplicatively to determine effort.

Georgopoulous, Mahoney, and Jones (1957) were among the first to test a cognitive theory of intention in an organizational setting. They showed that employee productivity could be predicted from the person's perceptions of the degree to which productivity leads to the attainment of personal goals.

While many of the studies of expectancy theory have provided moderate support for it, several drawbacks have been discovered. For example, it is doubtful whether people actually combine the variables in a multiplicative fashion as the theory suggests (Locke, 1975; Schmidt, 1973). Other criticisms are directed at errors in the validity of the theory itself (e.g., the ratio-scale problem). From a theoretical viewpoint, Locke (1975) and Staw (1977) criticized the underlying rationale of expectancy theory, namely, that people think rationally in regard to all aspects of their behavior, "when, in fact, we know that people have limited cognitive capabilities and that much of human behavior is habitual and subconscious" (Locke, 1975, p. 272). Similarly, Mitchell (1974) argued that expected-value approaches assume that people know all the alternatives, outcomes, and action-outcome relationships as well as how they feel about these outcomes. In most instances, however, people do not have all of the information assumed by this theory, nor do they use complex formulas in determining their actions (Mitchell, 1974). In summary, expectancy theory became so complex that it exceeded the measures that exist to test it (Dunnette, 1976).

Goal-Setting Theory

The underlying assumption of goal-setting theory is that people's intentions are a primary variable that explain their behavior. Once intentions are formed, they are the most immediate causes and predictors of behavior (Ryan, 1970).

Goal-setting theory states that assuming that a goal is accepted, specific, difficult goals lead to higher levels of performance than nonspecific—"do your best"—or easy goals (Locke, 1968; Locke & Latham, 1984). Furthermore, goals mediate the effects of variables such as feedback, praise, and money. Empirical research conducted in both laboratory and organizational settings provides strong support for these propositions (Latham & Lee, 1986; Latham & Yukl, 1975; Locke & Latham, 1984; Locke et al., 1981; Mitchell, 1979; Steers & Porter, 1974).

SOCIAL LEARNING THEORY

In contrast to reinforcement theory, which states that behavior is a function of its consequences; expectancy theory, which views people as cognitively striving to make decisions that will maximize valued outcomes; and goal-setting theory, which proposes that behavior is explained by a person's conscious intentions, social learning theory states that behavior is a function of a continuous reciprocal interaction among cognitive, behavioral, and environmental variables. That is, behavior both is determined by and affects environmental consequences, which in turn affect the person's conscious intentions or goals, and vice versa. Thus social learning theory provides a theoretical framework that encompasses the primary variables in cognitive and operant psychology—specifically, expectancies, anticipated outcomes, goal setting, and reinforcers. It differs from expectancy theory in that social learning theory is a relatively simple, pragmatic theory of human behavior unencumbered by mathematical equations and theorems.

Social learning theory emphasizes vicarious, symbolic, and self-regulatory processes in acquiring and maintaining behavior. Behavioral theories posit that learning can occur only by performing responses and experiencing their effects. Social learning theory enlarges this view by recognizing that people can learn vicariously by observing the behavior of others and its consequences for them. Through the use of symbols, people are able to foresee probable consequences, set goals, and act accordingly. Consequently, as a result of self-regulatory processes, people can learn to function as agents in their own self-motivation by rewarding progress toward goal attainment.

Empirical support for social learning theory has been obtained in well-controlled studies in experimental and clinical settings (Bandura, 1977a; Bromley & Shupe, 1979; Greenwald, 1980; Snyder, 1980). For example, considerable research has demonstrated that dysfunctional fears and inhibitions can be extinguished in a relatively short time using behavioral modeling techniques. This is achieved by having the phobic individual observe a model performing fear-provoking behavior without experiencing adverse consequences (Bandura, 1977a). In addition, empirical research has supported the prominent roles played by symbolic and self-regulatory processes in acquiring and maintaining changes in behavior (e.g., Bolles, 1972; Kanfer, 1975, 1980; Thoresen & Mahoney, 1974).

Behavior Modeling

During the past decade, one key aspect of social learning theory that has been investigated extensively in organizational settings is behavior modeling. Through the process of observing others, an individual learns how behaviors are performed and the consequences they produce (Bandura, 1977a). As a result, observational learning enables individuals to reduce time-consuming trial-and-error behaviors.

Moses and Ritchie (1976) evaluated the effectiveness of behavioral modeling in teaching AT&T supervisors interpersonal skills for dealing with employees. The data showed that the people who had been trained through the use of filmed models were rated by judges as more effective in role-playing simulations than people who had not received the training. Burnaska (1976) reported that supervisors at General Electric Company who participated in modeling training also received higher ratings on simulated role plays than untrained supervisors. Similarly, Byham, Adams, and Kiggins (1976) as well as Smith (1976) found that subordinates' perceptions of trained supervisors in interactions with them were more favorable than perceptions of untrained supervisors.

McGhee and Tuller (1978) criticized these studies with regard to their internal validity. In addition, they pointed out the possibility of criterion bias that may have occurred from the use of role-playing exercises both during training and again in the collection of the data. Finally, the use of role playing as a dependent variable raised questions regarding the external validity of two of these studies. Latham and Saari (1979) overcame these problems in a study involving first-line supervisors at Weyerhaeuser Company. Measurement criteria (reaction, learning, behavior, and outcome measures) for evaluating behavioral modeling were established prior to training, a control group was used, and a follow-up measure of performance on the job was assessed. This study provided strong support for the use of behavior modeling training programs in industry for bringing about a relatively permanent change in employee behavior (Goldstein, 1980; Wexley, 1984).

Self-Management

While modeling can facilitate self-management, the two concepts are not to be used interchangeably. Self-management is a technique in which the individual actively manipulates both reinforcers and punishers (Bandura, 1977a). Modeling differs in that the primary emphasis is on observational learning and does not include the use of self-monitoring or self-contracting techniques for acquiring and maintaining behaviors.

Training in self-management teaches an individual to assess what the problem is, establish a specific goal(s), monitor the ways in which the environment is hindering the attainment of the goal(s), determine whether the intervention is successful, and refine or change tactics when necessary (Kanfer, 1970; Kanfer & Karoly, 1972).

Training in self-management has only recently received attention in the organizational and human resource management literature for increasing employee effectiveness. Most of the advocates (e.g., Andrasik & Heimberg, 1982; Brief & Aldag, 1981; Luthans & Davis, 1979; Manz & Sims, 1980) have focused on Bandura's (1977a) social learning theory. Luthans and Davis (1979), for example, demonstrated the effectiveness of self-management techniques with managers in advertising, retailing, and manufacturing. The managers' self-monitoring and self-rewarding procedures for overcoming such problems as spending too much time on the phone, leaving one's own work to assist others, and failing to get to work on time were effective in changing the behavior. A limitation of case study research, however, is a threat to both the internal and external validity of the findings (Campbell & Stanley, Cook & Campbell, 1979).

Thus while various case studies (Luthans & Davis, 1979) and conceptual frameworks (e.g., Manz & Sims, 1980) have been presented in the management literature, there remains little in the way of empirical investigations of this training in organizational settings, a fact which served as the initial incentive to conduct the research on self-management and employee absenteeism. Consequently, the variables that have been implemented in clinical psychological studies are reviewed as a basis for designing and evaluating self-management training in the work setting.

TRAINING IN SELF-MANAGEMENT

Kanfer's model of self-regulation offers a practical framework for teaching self-management skills. Key variables in the model include goal setting, self-monitoring, and self-evaluation. Most self-management programs combine these techniques into one treatment package for studying behavioral problems in clinical settings (Kanfer, 1975, 1980; Karoly & Kanfer, 1982). For example, much of the outcome research on obesity has employed a "treatment package strategy" (Kazdin & Wilson, 1978). In this strategy, multiple variables are administered as part of a single program that is compared to a no-treatment situation. The underlying assumption is that the treatment package should "include as many component procedures as seem necessary to obtain, ideally, a total treatment success" (Azrin, 1977, p. 144). Moreover, if a treatment package proves effective, the researcher can undertake subsequent experimental analyses to evaluate the reasons for the success and thereby refine and enhance both the efficiency and the effectiveness of the treatment. This would not appear to be necessary, however, with regard to training in self-management.

Self-monitoring and self-evaluation, for example, are forms of feedback. Latham, Mitchell, and Dossett (1978) found that feedback by itself—without goal setting—had no effect on behavior following a performance appraisal. Similar findings were obtained in the clinical psychological literature by Simon (1979), who showed that self-monitoring in the absence of goal setting has no effect on behavior whatsoever. In fact, when self-monitoring is used alone, its effects are at best short-lived (Watson & Tharp, 1981). Erez (1977) found that goal setting in the absence of feedback had no effect on behavior. Locke and his colleagues (1981) concluded that both goal setting and feedback are critical for bringing about a long-term behavior change. Thus organizational psychologists such as Campbell (1982) have argued against trying to separate the effects of feedback, reinforcers, and goal setting.

Based on this literature review, the following variables were combined into a self-management training program rather than manipulated independently: goal setting, self-monitoring, self-reinforcement and/or punishment, self-formulation of a behavioral contract, and self-managing strategies for maintaining the desired behavior change. The purpose of this training was to examine its effects on employee attendance.

Because of the difficulties in controlling absenteeism (e.g., see Goodman & Atkin, 1984; Latham & Napier, 1984; Rosse & Miller, 1984; Steers & Rhodes, 1978, 1980, 1984), a treatment package was considered crucial to training success in bringing about a relatively permanent behavior change. The theory underlying the training was social learning theory. The hypothesized intervening variables were self-efficacy and outcome expectancies.

Nicholson and Johns (1985) have argued that despite the methodological sophistication and theoretical complexity of current research on absenteeism relative to the work of even 20 years ago, "it is doubtful how much wiser we are about the causes of absence" (Nicholson & Johns, 1985, p. 339). The underlying assumption of the present study is that the psychological variables affecting job attendance are one's perceived self-efficacy and outcome expectancies.

Self-Efficacy

A primary variable in social learning theory is self-efficacy. As noted earlier, self-efficacy is defined as an individual's judgment of his or her capabilities to organize and execute courses of action required to attain certain types of performances (Bandura, 1986). These expectations regarding personal mastery determine whether people will try to cope with difficult situations. In addition, efficacy expectations serve to determine how much effort people will expend and how long they will persist in their efforts to overcome obstacles or aversive events. The stronger the efficacy expectations, the more active one's efforts (Bandura, 1982, 1986).

Efficacy judgments vary on three dimensions—magnitude (or level), generality, and strength—all of which have important performance implications (Bandura, 1977b; 1986). Magnitude of self-efficacy is a function of the perceived level of difficulty of the tasks or situation at hand. Generality refers to an individual's overall sense of self-efficacy with regard to a particular set of behaviors. People may judge themselves as efficacious only in certain performance situations or across a wide range of activities and situations. Strength refers to the effort an individual will put forth in a situation. Self-knowledge about one's efficacy, whether accurate or faulty, is a synthesis of information from a variety of sources including performance attainments, observations, verbal inputs, and emotional states. Behavior change programs are said to be effective to the extent that they alter relevant efficacy expectations (Bandura, 1977b, 1982).

In contrast to self-efficacy, the predictive ability of outcome expectancies has not always been supported. For example, Godding and Glasgow (1985) conducted two studies to develop and evaluate the usefulness of self-efficacy and outcome expectancy measures in predicting smoking behavior. The sample were subjects who were chronic smokers participating in controlled smoking treatment programs. In both studies, self-efficacy correlated significantly with the amount of each cigarette smoked and the number of cigarettes smoked. Post-test efficacy ratings correlated highly with follow-up measures of smoking behavior six months later. On the other hand, outcome-expectancy scores did not increase the amount of variance accounted for in the dependent variables when combined with self-efficacy scores. This pattern of results is consistent with the findings of other studies involving such diverse activities as phobias, assertiveness, athletic feats, sales performance, and pain tolerance (Barling & Abel, 1983; Barling & Beattie, 1983; Lee, 1984; Manning & Wright, 1983). However, as Godding and Glasgow (1985) have noted, confusion over the meaning and specificity of both of these constructs may have confounded these findings.

Another controversy is the similarity of the self-efficacy construct to other cognitive influences on self-regulatory behavior, namely, instrumentalities, self-esteem, and locus of control (Bandura, 1984; Eastman & Marzillier, 1984). Bandura (1986) has argued that "self theories" are concerned with global self-images that detract from their power to explain and predict how people are likely to behave in particular situations. Examination of the concepts of self-efficacy and outcome expectancy suggests that they are similar to the concepts of effort-performance expectancy and instrumentality in expectancy theory (Vroom, 1964). Both self-efficacy and effort-performance expectancy represent beliefs about being able to perform a behavior. Outcome expectancy and instrumentality represent beliefs about the consequences of the behavior resulting in desirable or undesirable outcomes (Vroom, 1964). However, the concept of self-efficacy is broader than the expectancy concept in that self-efficacy includes such factors as beliefs about one's ability to function under stress, skill, ingenuity, and adaptability (Bandura, 1982; Bandura, 1986).

Two other constructs that also appear to be similar to self-efficacy are self-esteem and locus of control. Self-esteem (Korman, 1970, 1976) is defined as the extent to which an individual believes that he or she is a worthwhile and deserving individual. Locus of control (Rotter, 1966) refers to causal beliefs about outcome expectancies.

Bandura (1982, 1986) argued that self-esteem pertains to the evaluation of one's self-worth, which depends in part on cultural norms and individual perceptions regarding the value of the attributes one possesses. In contrast, perceived self-efficacy is concerned with the judgments of personal capabilities or competencies. For example, individuals may regard themselves as highly efficacious in an activity from which they derive no pride (e.g., consuming alcohol) or judge themselves inefficacious at an activity without suffering a loss of self-worth (for example, bowling).

Similarly, Bandura (1986) argued that locus of control (Rotter, 1966) refers to causal beliefs about the relation between actions and outcomes rather than about personal efficacy. For example, people who regard outcomes as personally determined would experience low self-efficacy and view the activities with a sense of futility. A student, for instance, who expects the course grade to be dependent entirely on skill in the subject matter but perceives that he or she lacks the necessary skill to pass the course (e.g., an understanding of multivariate statistics), may react in this way. A person's convictions that outcomes are determined by one's own actions can be demoralizing or encouraging, depending upon the person's level of perceived self-efficacy (Bandura, 1986).

In summary, outcome expectancies can be affected by efficacy judgments, and combinations of high and low levels of both types of expectancies will produce different patterns of behavior and affective states (Bandura, 1982, 1986; Lee, 1984). Recently, researchers (e.g., Bandura, 1986; Lee, 1985) have advocated the need to integrate mechanisms for altering personal feelings of efficacy as well as beliefs in the effectiveness of the desired behavior changes in the environment when implementing training programs designed to produce changes in behavior. For example, if individuals could observe and then participate in the behavior themselves, while discovering that there are minimal or no negative consequences when the behavior is performed, this could serve to increase outcome expectations in addition to judgments of self-efficacy (Bandura, 1986). One method that should be effective in increasing percepts of self-efficacy—and may be effective for altering outcome expectancies—is training in self-management. The underlying assumption of this study is that the two psychological variables affecting attendance and absenteeism are self-efficacy and outcome expectancies (Bandura, 1986; Lee, 1985).

ATTENDANCE

As noted elsewhere, self-management training has been effective in helping people to improve their study habits (Glynn, 1970; Richards, 1976), control their weight (Mahoney, Moura, & Wade, 1973), overcome depression (Tharp, Watson, & Wade, 1974), and modify their sexual preference (Kanfer & Phillips, 1970). The premise of this study was that training in self-management should also help the individual overcome perceived problems affecting attendance on the job.

Absenteeism continues to be a problem for researchers as well as managers. "A heavy investment of research effort on absenteeism has failed to generate significant dividends, whether one's criterion is the prediction, explanation, or control of absence" (Johns & Nicholson, 1982, p. 128). Two issues that have plagued absence research have been a lack of theory and methodological problems.

Theoretical Issues

A theoretical model for studying attendance was developed by Steers and Rhodes (1978). Attendance behavior is seen as a function of the motivation to attend and the ability to attend work. An underlying premise of the model is that absence behavior reflects both positive and negative forces that operate in an individual's life space.

A major limitation of this model is the failure of empirical research to support it (Mowday, Porter, & Steers, 1982). Three alternative theoretical perspectives of absence behavior have been presented by Johns and Nicholson (1982), Fichman (1984), and Rosse and Miller (1984).

Nicholson and his colleagues (Chadwick-Jones, Nicholson, & Brown, 1982; Johns & Nicholson, 1982) proposed a social or cultural view of absence. In brief, they argued that absenteeism levels reflect the social exchange within an organization in terms of agreed-upon behavior. An employee's decision to be absent or to come to work conforms to a normative level existing in the organization. Thus absenteeism is viewed as a social phenomenon. This theory, they argued, is in sharp contrast to traditional psychological approaches (e.g., approach-avoidance behavior, adjustment process, habit), which explain absenteeism as a result of an individual's unique problems. However, this approach offers little to the person who wishes to overcome, change, or resist group norms and values.

Fichman (1984) argued that absenteeism is a dynamic form of motivated behavior. Consequently, in order to explain an absence, one needs to know the full set of behavioral options in the individual's life space (i.e., both in work and nonwork settings). Thus absenteeism is only one specific element of a broad family of behaviors that might be termed attendance behaviors, adaptation, or withdrawal. The chief limitation of Fichman's theory is that the generality of assumptions about absence behavior and the complexity of relationships (e.g., expected rates of switching from one behavioral response to another) make it difficult to operationalize, let alone test, the propositions in the model (Hulin, 1984).

In a similar vein, Rosse and Miller (1984) argued that employees make varying responses in their attempt to adapt to the work environment. Withdrawal represents a subset of this general theoretical family. Depending on the outcome of these selected responses, the choice of behavior is either repeated at the next opportunity or eliminated. Thus Rosse and Miller (1984) argued that behavior choices are made to reduce anxiety, pain, stress, or dissatisfaction with the job.

There is a similarity between this argument and Hull's (1943) drive reduction theory. Therefore, the theory proposed by Rosse and Miller (1984) is subject to similar criticism. For example, there are people who come to work despite the fact that they are experiencing dissatisfaction, stress, anxiety, and so forth. They do so, moreover, in an attempt to rebel against or protest that which they perceive is causing them to have these feelings of dissatisfaction (Goodman & Atkin, 1984). In addition, Hamner, Landau, and Stern (1981) found that situations (e.g., coworker harassment) can occur in an organization where dissatisfaction actually increases pressure to come to work, yielding a positive correlation between employee attendance and employee dissatisfaction with the workplace.

Methodological Problems

A major methodological problem in research on absenteeism is its measurement. Various measures of absenteeism (e.g., total days lost, number of instances of absence) do not covary (Nicholson 1976). Although available data suggest that a frequency measure is preferable to a time-lost measure (Hamner & Landau, 1981), other researchers (e.g., Chadwick-Jones et al., 1971; Watson, Driver, & Watson, 1985) have argued that both frequency and time lost are important measures of absence and have reported correlations between the two measures of .61 and .71, respectively. Nevertheless, the test-retest reliabilities of these measures have typically been relatively low. For example, Muchinsky (1977) reported reliability estimates ranging from .00 to .74, with a median of .38. Such low reliabilities raise doubts as to the validity of reported findings where a measure of absenteeism was used as the dependent variable (Hamner & Landau, 1981; Steers & Rhodes, 1984).

In addition, there is disagreement concerning the very attempts to measure the absence of a behavior (i.e., not coming to work) versus the presence of a behavior (i.e., coming to work). Latham and Pursell (1975, 1977) showed that measuring employee attendance yields test-retest reliability estimates of .90. With respect to validity, Latham and Napier (1984) argued that the attendance criterion measures what it purports to measure, namely, whether the person is on the work site. To the extent that an absenteeism measure is also reliable, an attendance measure should correlate highly with it (e.g., − 1.0). This will rarely be the case, however, because of recorder bias in classifying the reason for an absence (Goodman & Atkin, 1984; Latham & Napier, 1984; Latham & Pursell, 1975).

The advantages of using attendance as a dependent variable are that (1) the measure is countable, (2) it is discrete, and (3), most important, unlike absenteeism, it is relatively unaffected by recorder judgment: a person either is or is not at work. An attendance measure does not depend on the classification judgments of supervisors as to the reasons why a person is not on the job (Fichman, 1984). Avoiding this issue is important because of the attributions that are made when a supervisor is required to interpret a nonevent (Fichman, 1984; Goodman & Atkin, 1984).

Ilgen (1977) argued that an attendance measure is obtuse because it is incapable of isolating the absenteeism subset of interest. Smulders (1980) extended this argument by asserting that an attendance measure gives information neither on frequency per employee nor on the duration of the spells. Both authors argued the need to distinguish between absenteeism per se and absenteeism for good reason. However, to the present writer's knowledge, no one has ever done this, including Ilgen and Smulders. Researchers almost always accept the existing supervisory classification system. This is because it is exceedingly difficult for them to observe employees off the job during intervals when they were scheduled to be at the work site.

Much less attention has been given to another serious problem in absence data, namely, non-normal sample distributions (Hamner & Landau, 1981; Terborg et al., 1982). The deviations from normality found in most samples of absence data place limitations on the use of statistical analyses in hypothesis testing and on the interpretations that can be made from such analysis (Wolpin & Burke, 1985). For example, if a test assumes a normal probability distribution for a dependent variable and that variable has a truncated or skewed distribution, the test may lead to invalid inferences and conclusions (Neter & Wasserman, 1974). In a recent study, Watson, Driver, and Watson (1985) demonstrated that threats to statistical conclusion validity in absence studies can be reduced by applying methods for inducing or testing for multivariate and univariate normality when using either multiple or single measures of absenteeism. Other researchers (e.g., Mardia, 1971), however, maintain that some statistical methods often result in valid conclusions even though the assumptions of the tests are not met exactly. In these cases, the robustness of non-normality is supported by the central-limit theorem (Mardia, 1971; Clegg, 1983).

In addition, Steers and Rhodes (1978) indicated that the failure to account for several alternative absenteeism measures is a major weakness in the research on absenteeism. Steers and Rhodes (1978) as well as Cummings (1981) have called for multivariate analyses in absenteeism studies in an effort to increase our conceptual understanding of the absence phenomenon. Although multivariate analyses will often assume normality, the results from Watson and colleagues (1985) suggest that methods for inducing or testing for multivariate normality can enhance the validity in absenteeism studies.

In light of these arguments, both attendance and absenteeism data were collected in the two studies to be discussed. Attendance was defined as the person being on the work site when he or she was scheduled to be there. The absenteeism measure reflected the current recording system used in the organization. Both variables were measured in terms of hours on or off the job.

Measures of both attendance and absenteeism were collected in order to minimize the probability of making a Type II error. In these series of studies, a Type II error would be made if the data suggested that the self-management training was not effective in reducing absenteeism when, in actuality, it was. In addition, it was anticipated that a measure of absenteeism might explain why people increased or decreased their attendance. Finally, multiple operationalism of the same dependent variable provides an estimate of the construct validity of the phenomenon of interest.

SUMMARY

Chapter 2 reviews behavioral theories (drive, operant conditioning) and cognitive theories (expectancy, goal setting) as precursors to social learning theory (behavior modeling, self-management). The chapter sets out the self-management training program components—goal setting, monitoring, self-reinforcement and self-punishment, formulation of contract, and maintenance strategies. The importance of the self-efficacy factor is noted, as are the advantages in using attendance, not absenteeism, as a dependent variable.

3

EVIDENCE THAT SELF-MANAGEMENT WORKS: RECENT RESEARCH

INTRODUCTION

As noted in Chapter 2, the implicit theory of absenteeism in both studies that are the subject of this chapter bases itself on self-efficacy. Many people perceive themselves as unable to overcome problems that interfere with their job attendance because they have low self-efficacy. Indirect support for this argument can be found in the revision of the Steers and Rhodes model (1984). These authors introduced perceived inability to come to work as a critical variable affecting employee attendance.

Bandura (1977b, 1978b, 1982) has argued the need to differentiate between self-efficacy and outcome expectancies. Whereas self-efficacy refers to beliefs regarding one's ability to overcome obstacles, outcome expectancies refer to beliefs concerning the extent to which one's responses will produce favorable or unfavorable outcomes. Behavior is less likely to be affected when people believe that they personally can overcome obstacles regarding coming to work but that the environment (e.g., supervisors, coworkers) will be unresponsive to their behavior change. Therefore, outcome expectancies were also examined as an intervening variable in terms of their effect on employee attendance. The training in self-management focused on ways that people can manipulate their environment to produce favorable consequences.

FIRST STUDY

The initial study examined the effects of training in self-management on self-efficacy, outcome expectancies, and job attendance. The effectiveness of the training was evaluated in terms of reaction, learning, cognitive self-reports, and behavioral criteria. The hypotheses were that people would act as follows:

1. Perceive the training to be effective (reaction criteria)
2. Acquire knowledge on how to overcome obstacles preventing them from coming to work (learning criteria)
3. Increase their self-efficacy and outcome expectancies (cognitive mastery)
4. Most importantly, increase their attendance on the job (behavioral criteria)

Systems theory (Lewin, 1938, 1947) states that variables other than the criterion of interest may be affected by an intervention. Therefore, measures of turnover and tardiness were collected to determine whether they too were affected by training in self-management to come to work. Because the training did not focus directly on these areas, no hypotheses were made with regard to these dependent variables. However, there is evidence that training in self-management skills sometimes generalizes to areas other than the primary dependent variables of interest (e.g., Ford, 1981).

In summary, the hypotheses of the initial study were that training in self-management increases job attendance and that the intervening variables that explain the effectiveness of this training are self-efficacy and outcome expectancies. Thus it was hypothesized that both cognitive variables must be perceived as favorable by the employee if job attendance is to increase significantly.

The training program was conducted because a needs analysis of the client organization revealed that absenteeism had become an increasingly important problem despite previous organizational attempts to decrease the amount of employee sick leave. The training program was explained to all employees, regardless of attendance rates, as a positive attempt by management to offer training to people who wanted to learn to manage their own behavior effectively. The intent was to minimize the stigma that might have been attached to a "disciplinary" program.

Method

Sample

A meeting was held with a director of personnel and a union representative to explain how training in self-management would be a positive approach to understanding and reducing employee sick leave so as to increase job attendance. The union representative agreed to support the training if the following conditions were agreed upon by management: (1) no employee would be required to receive the training and (2) no monetary incentives would be offered for increasing one's attendance. Agreement was reached on these conditions and a contract was signed indicating union support for the training.

A memo (Figure 3.1) was subsequently sent to all employees (n = 824) informing them of a training program on the self-management of employee attendance. The memo explained that the training would be sponsored by the organization's personnel department and offered on company time and that participation would be voluntary.

In an attempt to avoid the attrition rates reported in other self-management studies (e.g., Beneke & Harris, 1972), the memo stressed that only persons who would commit themselves to eight weekly one-hour group sessions and eight weekly 30-minute individual sessions should enroll in the training. Further, any individual scheduled for a vacation leave during the eight weeks of training should not enroll at this time.

One hundred and sixty three people responded to the memo. Of this number, 50 people were contacted. These people were selected on the basis of having used 50 percent or more of their sick leave hours during the last 12 months but not as yet having been placed on probation. Of the 50 individuals who were invited to attend the introductory meeting on self-management, 42 volunteered to receive the training. Of this number, two individuals stated that they would not be able to attend the eight weekly sessions due to scheduled vacation time. Thus they were not included in this study. The remaining 40 employees were randomly assigned to an experimental

Figure 3.1
Memo

Self-Management Course

I. Our organization is currently considering the concept of self-management.

II. We want to see if it can be applied to employee attendance.

    A. Why?

        1. It is a concern that employees from the top down share.

        2. Absenteeism costs all of us $$.

        3. Absenteeism disrupts the schedules of others.

        4. People who are here end up working harder rather than smarter.

        5. Attendance is critical to becoming self-managed crews.

        6. Self-management is a way for us to take a positive approach rather than a negative one.

III. How does it work?

    A. You would meet one hour a week for eight weeks—both in a group and in a one-on-one setting with a specialist in human resources from the Business School.

    B. Confidentiality is assured.

    C. The approach involves learning a set of skills to solve problems and manage your own behavior.

    D. The key to this training is that it is one-on-one as well as in groups, so that solutions are tailor-made for each participant.

    E. The course will be held on shift.

IV. Why should you consider this course?

    A. You will learn problem-solving skills.

        1. The skills are applicable to home as well as the job. They can be applied to smoking, weight loss, time management, self-motivation, stress management.

    B. You will improve your attendance by learning to cope with:

        1. Issues at home

        2. Problems at work

V. How do you sign up for this course?

    A. Contact your supervisor.

    B. You will receive information soon after that regarding the course meetings, when and where they will be held.

    C. It should be helpful as well as fun.

(n = 20) or a control group (n = 20). The people in the control group were told that they would be trained at a later date.

The mean age of the 40 employees was 44.33 years (SD = 11.4). Seventy percent of the employees were male. The mean number of years they had worked for the organization was 7.41 years (SD = 3.14). The individuals were employed by a state government as carpenters (n = 13), electricians (n = 14), and painters (n = 13).

Procedure

The control group, like the experimental group, was exposed to the ongoing organizational sanctions imposed for violating the absentee-ism policy. Thus they, like the experimental group, continued to receive attention from management. These sanctions consisted of the following steps: The supervisor issued a verbal warning to the offending employee for repeated absenteeism. If the person's job attendance did not improve, the employee received a written warning. If the written warning was not effective, the person was subject to a three-month probationary period. At the end of three months, the employee's attendance was reviewed to determine whether the probation should be terminated or whether the person should be dismissed from the organization.

The incentive for coming to work included the following: Each employee could earn 8 hours of sick leave each month for a total of 96 hours per year. Any hours that were not used during a given year were automatically transferred to the employee's balance for the following year. In addition, individuals were awarded compensation upon retirement for the total number of sick leave hours not used. This policy had been in effect for 12 years prior to and during this study.

The presence of this policy coupled with the desire of the people in the control group to increase their attendance provided a highly conservative test of the effectiveness of training in self-management. Evidence that the people in the control group wanted to increase their job attendance was inferred from their attendance at the intro-ductory session on self-management and their cooperation at various times throughout the study in filling out the questionnaires distributed by the trainer.

The supervisors of the trainees participated in a brief orientation session where the purpose and methodology of training in self-management were reviewed. The purpose of this session was to clarify the objectives of the training and to encourage a supportive climate in which the program would be recognized and supported by the immediate supervisors. The employees in the experimental group met for a one-hour training session each week for eight consecutive weeks. In addition, they met individually with the trainer for 30 minutes each week following the group session. The purpose of the individual meetings was to tailor the training to the specific concerns of each individual.

The training content consisted of lectures, group discussions, case studies, and the individualized sessions. The case studies (Figure 3.2) were developed by the investigator as a result of informal interviews with supervisors (n = 12) and employees (n = 13) prior to the training regarding obstacles that they believed prevented people from coming to work.

The group sessions focused on the following topics:

1. Orientation: self-management principles
2. Self-assessment
3. Goal setting
4. Self-monitoring
5. Self-evaluation (self-reinforcement and self-punishment)
6. Contracts
7. Maintenance, or relapse prevention
8. Review

Each training session presented a sequence of activities.

1. The trainees met with the trainer in groups of ten.
2. The trainer introduced the topic.
3. A case study that depicted an individual with a specific job attendance problem was presented to the trainees, who in turn developed solutions utilizing various self-management skills.
4. The trainees practiced the specific techniques that were emphasized in the respective session.
5. A homework assignment was given to prepare for the following meeting.

TRAINING SESSIONS

Each session concluded with a review of the learning points summarized during the session. In the interest of providing a sense of the overall range and scope of the eight-week training program, this

Figure 3.2
Case Studies Overview

Each week a different case problem will be presented to the group. After reviewing the technique for that training session, we will break up into smaller groups, discuss the case problem, and arrive at solutions using the self-management techniques presented in class that day. Each group will have an opportunity to present its solution and formulate a strategy for effectively managing the attendance problem presented.

Below is a list of topics that each case study will cover.

Case 1: Self-Assessment

Case 2: Goal Setting

Case 3: Self-Monitoring

Case 4: Self-Reward/Self-Punishment

Case 5: Behavioral Contracts

Case 6: Maintenance/Relapse Prevention

chapter takes up Sessions 1 and 8. Sessions 2 through 7 appear in considerable detail in Chapter 5.

Session 1: Orientation

The trainees were asked for their reasons for volunteering to receive the training. Their responses fell into one or more of the following categories:

1. Dissatisfaction with the current policies regarding absenteeism (i.e., they were viewed as punitive)
2. Acknowledgement of having problems attending work
3. A desire to learn self-management skills for these behaviors as well as other problem behaviors trainees were currently experiencing (e.g., excessive smoking, weight problems).

The underlying assumptions and rationale of self-management techniques (Figures 3.3 and 3.4) were then explained to the trainees. Measures of self-efficacy and outcome expectancies were taken. These measures were taken again immediately after, three months after, and six months after the training. A learning test was also administered during this session, three months after, and again six

Figure 3.3
Orientation: Self-Management Principles

1. Self-management is an effort by an individual to control his or her own behavior.
2. The techniques to be learned by the individual concentrate on the behaviors the individual performs.
3. The primary emphasis of self-management training is on improving behaviors through self-observation, goal setting, self-monitoring, self-reward and/or self-punishment, written contracts, and maintenance strategies.
4. The trainee designs and executes his or her own program.

Figure 3.4
Rationale of Training Program

A. Goal of the Program
   1. To train the individual to control his or her own behavior and achieve self-selected goals.
   2. To promote skills generalizable to other settings.

B. Format of the Program

   The training will consist of eight training sessions (one hour each week) in a group setting and eight individual sessions (one-half hour each week) with each participant. The purpose of the additional individual sessions will be to meet with each person on a one-to-one basis to tailor the program to his or her specific needs.

C. Role of the Trainer
   1. The goal of the investigator is to start a behavior change program that is carried out by the individual and to achieve changes that are maintained without external reinforcement.
   2. The role will be one of motivation, training, and support and maintenance (Kanfer, 1975).

D. Role of the Individual
   1. The individual will administer the self-management strategies and direct the change efforts with minimal assistance.
   2. The goal of the program with respect to the individual is to have that person control his or her own behavior and develop a set of coping skills applicable to other settings and situations.

Figure 3.4 (continued)

E. General Steps in Self-Management

1. Specify the target behavior in terms of behavior in a specific situation.

2. Make observations on how often the target behavior occurs, the antecedents that precede the behavior, and the consequences that follow it.

3. Form a plan to intervene by contingently reinforcing and/or punishing some desirable or undersirable behavior and by arranging situations to increase the chances of performing that behavior.

4. Maintain, adjust, and terminate the intervention program.

F. Characteristics of Self-Management

1. It concentrates on behaviors.

2. Heavy emphasis is placed on desirable behaviors and positive reinforcement.

3. The individual attempting self-management designs and executes his or her own program with initial minimal assistance.

Source: Adapted from "Self-Management Procedures," by F. Andrasik and J. Heimberg, 1982. In L. W. Frederiksen, ed., *Handbook of Organizational Behavior Management.* Copyright © 1982, by John Wiley & Sons, Inc. Reprinted by permission of John Wiley & Sons, Inc.

months after training. Each of these measures is shown later in this chapter.

Session 8: Review

During the last week of training, the trainer reviewed each technique presented in the program, answered questions from the trainees regarding these skills, and clarified expectations regarding the three-month and six-month evaluation period for assessing the effectiveness of the training. As previously noted, a measure of goal commitment was taken at the end of this session.

TRAINING EFFECTIVENESS

As noted earlier, the effectiveness of the training in self-management was evaluated in terms of reaction, learning, cognitive criteria, and behavioral criteria (Kirkpatrick, 1967). Each of these measures was used to evaluate different aspects of the effectiveness of training in self-management.

The reaction criteria measured how well the trainees liked the program with respect to its content, the techniques used, and the perceived relevance of the training to their needs. Learning criteria assessed the knowledge and skills that were acquired by the trainees (Wexley & Latham, 1981). Self-efficacy and outcome expectancies were measured in an attempt to identify the psychological variables that explain why the training was or was not effective in increasing job attendance and decreasing sick leave (behavioral criteria).

MANIPULATION CHECKS

Goal Commitment

Measures of the individual's commitment to the training consisted of a four-item questionnaire (Figure 3.5) administered to the trainees immediately after the eighth training session. The questionnaire contained five-point Likert-type items.

Use of Training Techniques

A primary concern was whether the trainees would use the skills that were taught in the training class. Measures of the individual's application of the various skills, including relapse prevention and maintenance, consisted of a five-point, 13-item questionnaire (Figure 3.6) administered to the trainees during the three-month and six-month follow-up sessions.

DEPENDENT VARIABLES

The four criteria for evaluating the effectiveness of the training were reaction measures, learning measures, measures of self-efficacy and outcome expectancies, and employee sick leave and attendance.

Reaction Measures

Measures of the individual's reactions to the training consisted of a five-item questionnaire (Figure 3.7) administered to the trainees immediately after the last training session, three months later, and again six months later. This permitted an assessment of the stability (test-retest reliability) of the trainee reactions. The questionnaire contained five-point Likert-type items.

Figure 3.5
Goal Commitment Measure

Place a checkmark next to the alternative that best describes your personal response to each item. Thank you for your cooperation.

1. Commitment to a goal means acceptance of it as your own personal goal and your determination to attain it. How committed were you to attaining the goal that was set?

    _____1   not at all committed

    _____2   slightly committed

    _____3   moderately committed

    _____4   very committed

    _____5   completely committed

2. How important was it to you to at least attain the goal that was set?

    _____1   not important

    _____2   of little importance

    _____3   somewhat important

    _____4   moderately important

    _____5   important

3. To what extent did you internally agree to strive to attain the goal that was set?

    none_____   a little_____   some_____   quite a bit_____   a lot_____
        1   2   3   4   5

4. How reasonable was the goal that you set?

    _____1   unreasonable

    _____2   slightly reasonable

    _____3   moderately reasonable

    _____4   very reasonable

    _____5   completely reasonable

Figure 3.6
Training Techniques Measure

1. What is your ideal goal for attendance? _____

2. What is a realistic attendance goal for? _____

3. What is the average number of days per week that you did daily self-monitoring of attendance during these months?

   _____ September _____ October _____ November _____ December

   _____ January _____ February _____ March

4. What is the average number of days per week that you used the techniques taught in the training sessions (other than self-monitoring) during these months?

   _____ September _____ October _____ November _____ December

   _____ January _____ February _____ March

5. If you stopped charting or using the other techniques taught in the program for a week or longer, how successful were you in returning to the entire program?

1	2	3	4	5
very unsuccessful	moderately unsuccessful	neutral	moderately successful	very successful

6. A major reason that I stopped self-monitoring and using the other techniques was that I wasn't keeping my goals, so I didn't want to chart my attendance.

1	2	3	4	5
strongly disagree	moderately disagree	neutral	moderately agree	strongly agree

7. A major reason that I stopped self-monitoring and using the other techniques was that I was satisfied with my attendance.

1	2	3	4	5
strongly disagree	moderately disagree	neutral	moderately agree	strongly agree

8. I believe that daily self-monitoring was helpful to me in increasing attendance.

1	2	3	4	5
strongly disagree	moderately disagree	neutral	moderately agree	strongly agree

Figure 3.6 (continued)

9. I believe that the social support obtained in the group was helpful to me in increasing attendance.

1	2	3	4	5
strongly disagree	moderately disagree	neutral	moderately agree	strongly agree

10. In the future, if you stop self-monitoring or using the other techniques taught in the class, how likely is it that you will be able to begin using them again?

1	2	3	4	5
very unlikely	moderately unlikely	neutral	moderately likely	very likely

11. In the future, a major reason that I would stop self-monitoring or using the other techniques taught in the program would be that I was satisfied with my job attendance.

1	2	3	4	5
strongly disagree	moderately disagree	neutral	moderately agree	strongly agree

12. How likely is it that you will eventually reach and maintain a satisfactory rate of attendance?

1	2	3	4	5
very unlikely	moderately unlikely	neutral	moderately likely	very likely

13. How likely is it that you will reach a satisfactory rate of attendance but not be able to maintain it?

1	2	3	4	5
very unlikely	moderately unlikely	neutral	moderately likely	very likely

Learning Measures

Learning measures were obtained before, three months after, and again six months after training. The trainees completed a ten-item situational test. The methodology was similar to that used in a situational interview (Latham et al., 1980; Latham & Saari, 1984). Each item was a description of a problem behavior that the person wished to change. The questions, developed by the author, were based on informal interviews with supervisors (n = 14) regarding obstacles preventing people from coming to work.

Figure 3.7
Reaction Measure

Directions: Circle the number that best exemplifies your answer to each of these questions. A space has been left underneath each question for any comments you would like to make.

1. The training I received helped me identify obstacles preventing me from coming to work.

    Disagree   1   2   3   4   5   Agree

---

2. The training I received helped me overcome obstacles preventing me from coming to work.

    Disagree   1   2   3   4   5   Agree

---

3. The training I received helped me to set goals to increase my attendance.

    Disagree   1   2   3   4   5   Agree

---

4. The training I received helped me to feel more confident about my ability to control my own behavior.

    Disagree   1   2   3   4   5   Agree

---

5. I believe this training should be given to other employees who have difficulty coming to work.

    Disagree   1   2   3   4   5   Agree

People in both the training group and the control group completed this test under uniform conditions with the trainer present as a monitor. Code numbers were used for identification so that the judges who scored the test would not know who had received the training. The judges included the trainer, the personnel training director, and a line manager.

In order to facilitate objective scoring, the judges developed a behavioral scoring guide (Latham, et al., 1980; Latham & Saari, 1984) for defining poor (1), average (3), and excellent (5) answers to each question prior to scoring. The complete test and the scoring guide are shown in Figures 3.8 and 3.9, respectively.

Figure 3.8
Learning Measure

---

1. I am absent a lot from work because I get colds and stay home. I met with my supervisor this morning and was told that I would be put on probation if this behavior continued. When asked why I always get sick, I thought it was a dumb question. What should I be doing?

2. I sometimes become "stressed" on the job because of unpleasant and repeated reprimands from my supervisor. Lately, I take a few hours of my sick leave, take off early, and have a few drinks at the local tavern. Family problems are surfacing as a result of my recent behavior. How can I manage my attendance on the job more effectively?

3. I'm missing too many days from work each month and my fellow employees are beginning to treat me coldly and complain that when I am not on the job, they must pick up the slack. In reality, my wife does not have sick leave benefits, so when the kids do get sick, I am the one who stays home to take care of them. What should I do?

4. I want to increase my attendance at work. I have identified what behaviors keep me from coming to work and what the consequences of these actions are. What should I do now?

5. I have been monitoring my attendance by keeping a daily record of whether I am at work or not. In the beginning, just keeping a record of my behavior made my attendance increase. Yet after two weeks, I am back to skipping work again. What am I doing wrong?

6. I like to go out and party on Thursday nights. For the past three months, I have gotten too bombed to make it into work on Friday. My supervisor has become very upset with me and suggested I do something about my recent behavior as it seems to be getting in my way of being effective on the job. What should I do?

7. The reason I don't come to work is that I do not get along with a particular person whom I work with. Whenever she is on shift, I call in sick. I noticed that when I do have contact with her on the job, we get into arguments because she constantly interrupts me while I am talking.

Figure 3.8 (continued)

I decided to set a goal of "getting along with her" but it does not seem to be working. What should I do?

8. I generated a list of reinforcers and punishers for meeting my goal of perfect attendance for one week. Each day I went to work, I would reward myself at the end of the day with a cold beer. If I did not go to work, I wouldn't eat supper that night. Last week, I missed two days, but ate dinner anyway. This week, I missed work again, but couldn't go without eating, so I skipped punishing myself again. What is my problem?

9. I have a problem coming to work sometimes because my car breaks down and I have no other way to get there. The last time this happened, I just called in sick to work and ended up doing things around the house all day. Today, I was reprimanded for being absent too much and my supervisor suggested that I better find myself a way to get to work. What should I do?

10. I am often unable to come to work because I can't find a permanent babysitter for my kids. They are too young to stay home alone and my regular babysitter has been on vacation for the last month. I tried calling a few other people but gave up and have been using my sick leave from time to time to stay home with the kids. My supervisors haven't said anything to me yet but I've noticed my peers at work being rather "cool" to me lately. What should I do to remedy my situation at home?

Figure 3.9
Behavioral Anchors Scoring Guide

QUESTION 1

1. Tell my supervisor the situation and hopefully he or she will understand why I need to be absent so frequently.

3. Set a goal to take better care of myself, perhaps by getting to bed earlier.

5. My first step will be self-assessment. I will make a list of all antecedents and consequences of the problem behavior and any thoughts or feelings I have regarding the situation. Then, I will set specific goals based on overcoming this behavior and ways to monitor and reward my accomplishments.

Figure 3.9 (continued)

QUESTION 2

1. Don't get into arguments with your supervisor.

3. Make a list of the reasons I am reprimanded by my supervisor and try to alter my behavior.

5. Assess the occurrence of the reprimands by my supervisor through the self-assessment technique. Work with my supervisor and offer suggestions to change the current situation. Then set goals based on my new pinpointed behavior.

QUESTION 3

1. If I have not been reprimanded by my supervisor for my attendance behavior, I will ignore the problem.

3. Set a goal to trade off staying home with my wife/husband.

5. Identify possible alternatives to the problem situation that I have identified. For example, I should set a goal to find a permanent babysitter for my children so that in the event they get sick, someone will be at home to watch them and I will not have to take a day off from work.

QUESTION 4

1. See if my attendance increases.

3. Identify a list of reinforcers and punishers based on the appropriate behaviors identified.

5. Begin setting goals based on the behaviors that I have identified. The initial step would require checking to see if I could rearrange or reorder any of the behaviors so that the consequences that reward not attending work can be changed to reward attending work instead.

QUESTION 5

1. I probably am not using the right self-monitoring device. I should change to another way of recording the behavior.

3. Begin recording my behavior again daily. As my attendance stabilizes over time, I can gradually stop self-monitoring.

5. I probably have not set goals for attending or not attending work. In addition, self-monitoring does not work permanently on its own. I need to reward myself when I meet my self-set goals and punish myself when I fail to meet my goals.

Figure 3.9 (continued)

QUESTION 6

1. Talk with my supervisor and say that I realize the seriousness of the situation and that I will make an effort to attend work after I have my Thursday nights out.

3. Change going out to another night of the week—either Friday or Saturday night, when I do not have to get up to go to work the next morning.

5. Begin with pinpointing the problem behavior (e.g., why am I going out drinking every Thursday night?). Once I have specifically defined the problem(s) and the situation(s) that it occurs in, analyze the antecedents to not coming to work and what consequences follow. Most importantly, make a list of my behaviors, feelings, and thoughts during these situations.

QUESTION 7

1. Go to my supervisor and explain why I am absent. If this is not sufficient, check into getting a transfer.

3. Reset my goal for specific days to try to get along with her. My goal is too vague right now.

5. My goal is too vague. I must break the goal down into specific observable behaviors in the various situations in which they occur. Also, I may want to observe our behavior to make sure I have correctly identified the antecedents and the consequences of my problem behavior.

QUESTION 8

1. Nothing is wrong, If I must eat dinner, I am going to eat. I will keep trying.

3. Reset my goal and re-analyze the punisher that I am currently using. If I must use this punisher, change the frequency of the punishment to once a week rather than daily.

5. The punisher is too aversive to do any good. Eating dinner is a necessary function and too much a necessity to give up totally. I should generate another list of more reasonable punishers.

QUESTION 9

1. Simply get my car fixed, and then I will be prepared to get to work.

3. Rent a car until my car gets fixed and maybe pick up a bus schedule to consider whether taking the bus during these times may serve as an alter-

Figure 3.9 (continued)

native mode of transportation.

5. Begin my self-assessment by pinpointing the problem behavior and ask-ing myself what actually keeps me from coming to work. Then I would do an A-B-C analysis of the events that lead me to stay home and the consequences that follow my decision to remain home. I would target in on the consequences of this decision.

QUESTION 10

1. I would explain the situation to my supervisor. He or she should under-stand that child care is important.

3. Make a list of alternative places I could leave my children or additional people who could babysit for me.

5. Since I have identified the problem in my situation, set a goal to find at least three available babysitters for my children. Contact all three, hire one of them and arrange to keep at least two of the other individuals as possible sitters if the recently hired one should get sick. Alternatives are important in this situation.

Cognitive Measures

Self-efficacy and outcome expectancy questionnaires were administered to each individual before, immediately after, three months after, and again six months following the training. The self-efficacy questionnaire was developed based on two dimensions that are viewed by Bandura (1977a) as critical for assessing efficacy judgments, namely, level and strength (Bandura, 1977a). As noted in Chapter 2, level refers to the difficulty of the tasks or situation at hand. Strength of perceived self-efficacy refers to the effort an individual will put forth in a situation.

The measure of self-efficacy used in this study (Figure 3.10) contained 15 items measuring people's beliefs about various obstacles and situations that may prevent them from coming to work. Similar scales have been used in training programs designed to teach individuals self-management skills for reducing cigarette smoking (e.g., DiClemente, 1981; Godding & Glasgow, 1985; Lichenstein & Condiotte, 1981) and improving performance in assertiveness tasks (Lee, 1984a). The items on this scale were generated from informal interviews with both supervisors (n = 13)

Figure 3.10
Self-Efficacy Measure

For each statement below, indicate whether you would be able to attend work in each of the situations described below (check yes or no). For each item that you check yes, rate your confidence (1-9); 1 being not confident at all; 5 being moderately confident; 10 being highly confident) in your ability to attend work in each specific situation.

1	2	3	4	5	6	7	8	9	10
highly unconfident				moderately confident					highly confident

YES/NO

1. When you are bored with your job.

    1   2   3   4   5   6   7   8   9   10

2. When you are sick.

    1   2   3   4   5   6   7   8   9   10

3. When you are hung over.

    1   2   3   4   5   6   7   8   9   10

4. When you feel stressed.

    1   2   3   4   5   6   7   8   9   10

5. When you have car trouble.

    1   2   3   4   5   6   7   8   9   10

6. When you are having family problems.

    1   2   3   4   5   6   7   8   9   10

7. When you have no one to take care of your children.

    1   2   3   4   5   6   7   8   9   10

8. When your supervisor is upset with you.

    1   2   3   4   5   6   7   8   9   10

9. When you see others missing work with no penalty.

    1   2   3   4   5   6   7   8   9   10

10. When you want to sleep in.

    1   2   3   4   5   6   7   8   9   10

11. When you dislike your co-workers.

    1   2   3   4   5   6   7   8   9   10

12. When you want to spend time with the family.

    1   2   3   4   5   6   7   8   9   10

Figure 3.10 (continued)

```
13.  When attendance is not important to the organization.

     1      2      3      4      5      6      7      8      9      10

14.  When you are upset with a co-worker.

     1      2      3      4      5      6      7      8      9      10

15.  When you have a chance to engage in your favourite hobby.

     1      2      3      4      5      6      7      8      9      10
```

and personnel officers (n = 3) as well as from examination of employees' attendance records. The scale represented a variety of job attendance situations, ranging from rather innocuous types of events to those considered more stressful and difficult in nature (satisfying the criterion of magnitude or level).

For each of the 15 items, the trainees indicated whether they felt that they would be able to come to work in each of the job attendance situations described (efficacy level) and, if yes, rated their confidence separately on a scale from 0 to 100 (efficacy strength).

The outcome expectancy scale contained 15 items measuring anticipated negative and positive consequences for coming to work (e.g., "I will still receive criticism from my boss," "I will be perceived as a dependable employee"). The scale was adapted from previous scales used in outcome expectancy research (e.g., Davis & Yates, 1982; Barling & Abel, 1983) as well as from interviews with supervisors regarding attendance behavior and its associated outcomes.

For each item, individuals were asked to designate on a 100-point probability scale (expressed in % units), ranging in ten-unit intervals, the probability that they would experience or achieve a particular outcome as a result of coming to work. A summary score (ratings on positive items minus ratings on negative items) was derived for each individual as a means of assessing overall outcome expectancy. The questionnaire is shown in Figure 3.11.

Attendance and Absenteeism

Job attendance was defined as the number of hours on the job the employee was present when he or she was scheduled to be there. Absenteeism was defined by the organization as falling into one of 11

Figure 3.11
Outcome Expectancy Measure

People have different feelings about the consequences of their behavior. Below are some sentences that describe certain beliefs that people have about their chances of receiving or experiencing certain outcomes as a result of increasing their attendance on the job. For each item below, circle the number that indicates how you feel.

0	1	2	3	4	5	6	7	8	9
highly unlikely					moderately likely				highly likely

1. My supervisor will perceive me as a dependable employee.

   0   1   2   3   4   5   6   7   8   9

2. My co-workers will perceive me as competent.

   0   1   2   3   4   5   6   7   8   9

3. I will increase my sense of accomplishment.

   0   1   2   3   4   5   6   7   8   9

4. I will increase my chances of obtaining a promotion.

   0   1   2   3   4   5   6   7   8   9

5. I will increase my effectiveness on the job.

   0   1   2   3   4   5   6   7   8   9

6. I will still receive criticism from my boss.

   0   1   2   3   4   5   6   7   8   9

7. I will increase my level of stress.

   0   1   2   3   4   5   6   7   8   9

8. I will have to interact more with my co-workers.

   0   1   2   3   4   5   6   7   8   9

9. I won't have any time to spend with my family.

   0   1   2   3   4   5   6   7   8   9

10. I will have to reschedule my medical appointments for the weekend.

   0   1   2   3   4   5   6   7   8   9

11. I will have more work to do.

   0   1   2   3   4   5   6   7   8   9

12. My supervisor will still perceive me as incompetent.

   0   1   2   3   4   5   6   7   8   9

Figure 3.11 (continued)

```
13.   I will still receive boring job assignments.

      0     1     2     3     4     5     6     7     8     9

14.   I will not gain any additional recognition from my peers.

      0     1     2     3     4     5     6     7     8     9

15.   I will be more likely to receive a raise.

      0     1     2     3     4     5     6     7     8     9
```

categories: bereavement leave, civil duty leave, holiday leave, jury leave, leave without pay, maternity leave, military leave, military leave without pay, sick leave, vacation leave, and workmen's compensation leave.

Sick leave absenteeism was recorded as 49.8 percent of the total absenteeism in the organization. Thus this measure of absenteeism was of primary interest to the client organization. This measure was defined as the number of sick leave hours taken per employee. Both measures were divided by the total number of hours in the work week, namely, 40. None of the employees worked overtime.

The disadvantage of this measure of absenteeism from a theoretical perspective is similar to the disadvantage of a measure of attendance. Both measures ignore the difference between voluntary and involuntary absenteeism. Some people may take sick leave because they are too ill to come to work, while others may simply have negotiated with a supervisor to record a vacation day as sick leave (Goodman & Atkin, 1984). These two behaviors, illness and negotiation, are very different theoretically.

To overcome this problem, each person who stayed away from work would have to be observed, and the interobserver reliability of the observations would have to be calculated. To the author's knowledge, this has never been done in the research literature on absenteeism. Thus the present absenteeism measure conforms to research practice. A measure of attendance is also void of theory with regard to why people stay away from work. However, the two measures provide construct validity for the criterion of primary interest in this study, namely, employee presence at the work site.

From an empirical standpoint these two behavioral measures do not guard against a Type II error. To the extent that trainees in this study were physically incapacitated, training in self-management would not decrease sick leave nor increase job attendance. Thus the failure to distinguish between voluntary and involuntary sick leave provided a very conservative test of training in self-management.

Tardiness and Turnover

Tardiness was defined as the number of days in a given period on which the employee reported more than 15 minutes late for work. Turnover was measured by (1) the number of employees who quit and (2) the number of employees who were either asked to resign or were fired in each month the study was conducted.

Neither tardiness nor turnover were viewed by the client organization as a problem. The base rate in the organization was 2.8 percent and 4 percent, respectively. Thus these data were collected primarily to determine if the training program in self-management on attendance affected these behaviors adversely.

SECOND STUDY

Introduction

The purpose of the second study was twofold. First, it was conducted to determine the extent to which relapse occurred six months and nine months following the training in self-management. Relapse can be problematic in self-management training because the emphasis is on the individual rather than on the reinforcement of the newly acquired coping skills by people in the individual's environment. (Brownell et al., 1986). Relapse is obviously a problem when the culture in which the trainee is functioning does not support these behaviors.

The second purpose of this study was to test—by studying a second sample of employees—the hypothesis that perceived self-efficacy explains why people come or do not come to work. This was done by training the control group and comparing its performance with that of the original experimental group, and by correlating a measure of self-efficacy with subsequent job attendance.

Method

Sample

The employees in this study were those who were described by Frayne and Latham (1987). No turnover had occurred. These people (n = 40) were unionized state government employees employed as carpenters, electricians, and painters.

Procedure

As described by Frayne and Latham (1987), 20 of the 40 employees had been randomly assigned to a training situation in which they had been taught self-management skills for job attendance. Six months and nine months subsequent to the training, reaction, learning, cognitive, and behavioral measures were taken to evaluate the effects of the training over time. The purpose of the reaction measures was to assess whether employees' favorable attitudes toward the training diminished over time. In addition, the employees were interviewed to determine whether their reasons for absenteeism had changed.

The learning measures were collected to determine whether the employees retained the knowledge disseminated in the training program. If the knowledge was not retained, it could explain any return to pretraining levels of job attendance that occurred. The cognitive measure, perceived self-efficacy, was assessed to determine its importance as a psychological variable affecting job attendance. A decrease in the trainees' sense of self-efficacy would also explain any decrease in job attendance, assuming no change in knowledge retention. Finally, both job attendance and employee sick leave were measured. Sick leave was measured because it accounted for 49.8 percent of the organization's categorized reasons for absenteeism (Frayne & Latham, 1987). Measuring both job attendance and categorized sick leave permitted multiple operationalism of the dependent variable of primary interest, namely, employee presence at the work site.

Subsequent to the nine-month follow-up assessment, the employees in the control group received the identical training in self-management described by Frayne and Latham (1987). The only difference between the two studies was the trainer. Frayne conducted the first training program; a person in the organization's personnel department, trained by Frayne, conducted the replication study. The data for this second experiment were collected three months following the training. The results were compared with those collected from the original experimental group three months after it had been trained.

SUMMARY

Many people perceive themselves as unable to overcome problems that interfere with their job attendance; they have a low sense of self-efficacy. The studies under discussion examine the effects of self-management training on self-efficacy, outcome expectancies, and job attendance. The two studies involved eight weekly group sessions and eight weekly one-on-one sessions, covering orientation, self-assessment, goal setting, self-monitoring, self-evaluation, contracts, maintenance and relapse prevention, and review. The second study—identical to the first except for the trainer—bore out the hypothesis of the first, that perceived self-efficacy explains why people do or do not come to work.

4

RESEARCH RESULTS

Results from both research studies as well as the significance of these findings, both theoretical and practical, are the subject of this chapter.

DATA ANALYSIS

The distributions of the attendance and absenteeism measures were examined using measures of skewness (g1) and kurtosis (g2) (Hammer & Landau, 1981). According to Kendall and Stuart (1958), when g1 approaches 2 and g2 is greater than 5, there is considerable skewness and leptokurtosis. Extreme values disproportionately influence the properties of the sample distributions (means, variances) on which linear techniques such as correlation coefficients are built (Hamner & Landau, 1981; Wolpin & Burke, 1985). In the present data, neither the measure of attendance (g1 = 1.031; g2 = 3.658) nor the measure of absenteeism (g1 = 1.337; g2 = 2.857) violated these boundaries.

Bartlett's test of sphericity (determinant = .68345) was used to examine the correlation matrix of the measures of attendance and sick leave absenteeism. The test is based on the determinant of the within-cells correlation matrix. A determinant that is close in value to 0 indicates that one or more of the variables is correlated with the other dependent variables (Neter & Wasserman, 1974). The results of the test showed that the two variables (absenteeism and attendance) were not independent. Thus the use of multivariate analyses was appropriate (Winer, 1971).

Box's M test, which is based on the determinants of the variance-covariance matrices in each cell as well as on the pooled variance-covariance matrix, was used to test for the homogeneity of the matrices. The result of Box's M test (5.3487) revealed no reason to suspect the homogeneity-of-dispersion assumption.

The remaining dependent variables were tested for assumptions of normality and homogeneity of variance. Results of these analyses showed that none of the data were in serious violation of the assumptions of the respective statistical tests. Consequently, planned univariate and multivariate analyses of variance were conducted.

POWER ANALYSIS

A power analysis (Cohen, 1977) was conducted using a sample size of N = 40 and a significance criterion of α = .05. The power of a statistical test is the probability that it will yield statistically significant results. If the null hypothesis was rejected, omega squared was calculated. Omega squared is a measure of the proportion of variance in Y (the dependent variable) accounted for by X (the independent variable). Results and interpretation of each analysis were examined for each of the dependent variables and are presented in the criterion measures section found later in this chapter.

PRETRAINING DATA

Analysis of pretraining data failed to yield any significant differences on any of the dependent measures. The respective means and standard deviations are shown in Table 4.1.

MANIPULATION CHECKS

Goal Commitment

The coefficient alpha of a four-item commitment measure (e.g., "To what extent will you strive to attain the goal?" "How important

Table 4.1
Means and Standard Deviations for Pretraining Data

Measure	Training		Control	
	M	SD	M	SD
Attendance	32.2	7.6	33.1	5.6
Sick Leave	5.26	3.61	4.96	2.16
Learning	15.6	4.2	16.2	4.3
Self-Efficacy	45	14.3	46.4	13.2
Outcome Expectancy	28.6	8.1	30.15	9.82

is it to you to at least attain the goal that was set?'') administered during the final week of training in the Frayne and Latham study was .81; in the subsequent training of the replication group one year later, it was .84. The means of the responses to the five-point Likert-type items (M = 4.73, SD = .22; and M = 4.81, SD = .25) in the two samples were high and not significantly different.

Use of Training Techniques

A key concern was whether the trainees used the skills taught in the training class. A final questionnaire was administered at both the three-month and six-month follow-up periods to assess the individual's use of the techniques taught in the training, expectations for success in the future, and possible reasons for relapse.

The trainees responded to a five-point, 13-item questionnaire on the extent to which goals were being set, feedback charts were being maintained, and reinforcers andor punishers were being administered. The responses correlated significantly (p. <.05) with job attendance at the three-month follow-up period (.48, .45, .57, respectively) as well as at the six-month follow-up period (.44, .53, .62, respectively). Further corroboration that the trainees were applying the training content was obtained by the trainer's visual inspection of the feedback charts. Only three people were not keeping attendance charts systematically.

People who reported that they had been successful in returning to the program when they had stopped using the techniques for a while or who anticipated being able to return to the program after a future relapse were more likely to increase their attendance on the job (r =

.46, r = .59, r = .64, p < .05; three-month and six-month follow-up, respectively). People who anticipated being able to reach and maintain their attendance goals also tended to increase attendance (r = .67, p = .01; r = .76, p = .01; three-month and six-month follow-up, respectively). Similar results were obtained in the second study.

CRITERION MEASURES

Reaction Measures

Assessing the long-term reactions to the training was especially important because many trainees in the Frayne and Latham study had asserted during the first week of training that sick leave was a privilege that belonged to them. Thus it was important to determine whether the trainees' subsequent positive affect toward the program three months after the training was maintained. The five-point, five-item questionnaire (e.g., "The training I received helped me overcome obstacles preventing me from coming to work") used by Frayne and Latham was completed anonymously six months and nine months after the training had ended. The coefficient alphas were .78 and .75, respectively. The test-retest reliability coefficient between Month 3 and Month 9 was .83.

In the replication sample, the alpha was .74 three months after the training had occurred. This is comparable to the alpha of .73 obtained in the original three-months study. The test-retest reliability of the reaction measures over the three-month period in the original study was .81; in the replication study it was .84.

The employee reactions in the original training group assessed three months after the training had taken place (M = 4.46, SD = .41) remained highly positive six months later (M = 4.48, SD = .46) and nine months later (M = 4.47, SD = .43). The difference among these values is not statistically significant. Thus employee affect toward the training program remained highly positive.

The employee reactions in the replication sample three months after receiving the training from a different trainer was also high (M = 4.45, SD = .43). A t test revealed no significant difference between their highly positive attitude and that exhibited by the original training group (M = 4.43, SD = .49) three months after their training had taken place.

Despite the attempt to remove any stigma resulting from the

training being viewed as disciplinary or remedial in nature, the trainees initially expressed hostile feelings about their enrollment (e.g., "I guess we are the delinquent bunch," "You're in here too?" "Sick leave abuser!"). Their overt behavior consisted of fist fighting and name calling, which erupted during the first session as a result of derogatory remarks exchanged between two trainees regarding respective sick leave use.

During the course of the training, comments from the trainees indicated that they were enjoying the sessions and that attitudes were improving (e.g., "You know, we can't change our supervisors or the environment around this place, so maybe we should consider how to help ourselves," "Can you believe that I keep a bus schedule handy now in case I have car trouble?" "Hey, I haven't missed a day yet, how about you?").

One trainee who had come to each session in a slovenly fashion began taking interest in good grooming habits and appearance. During the fourth and fifth week of training, the trainee had commented several times during his individual sessions that he had begun to feel "better" about himself overall as a result of his enrollment and performance in the training and on the job. Other employees expressed looking forward to the training sessions and discussed progress with other trainees prior to the beginning of a training class.

In addition, at least three individuals reported using the self-management techniques for problems other than sick leave, namely, weight loss, smoking, and stress reduction. Anecdotal evidence revealed that these individuals also appointed members of the family (e.g., wife, son) to serve as external verification of progress in the program. During the six-month follow-up interviews, these individuals reported a 30-pound reduction in weight, a reduction of smoking from 2.5 packs per week to .5 packs per week, and a significant improvement in a personal relationship as a result of effective management of stressful situations, respectively. Two other individuals reported using the techniques for implementation of a body-building program and for managing financial expenses. These anecdotes support data on the generalizability of self-management to other behaviors (Bandura, 1982, 1986).

During the three-month follow-up of the initial study, interviews with supervisors (n = 12) revealed that they perceived both favorable attitude changes on the part of trainees and overall positive impact on those employees who had not enrolled in the training. Supervisors reported that the training was not only effective for self-management of sick leave but also for teaching individuals effective strategies for maintaining schedules of job shop work orders and job completion. In addition, supervisors observed several trainees sharing viewpoints regarding more effective ways of completing the work.

Similar reactions to the training were obtained from the supervisors (n = 12) during the sixth-month follow-up as well. In fact, one supervisor reported his personal satisfaction with two of the trainees' on-the-job performances and had recommended both of them for a project start-up.

Learning Measures

An important issue is to understand in what way the training was effective. One criterion is learning (Kirkpatrick, 1967; Wexley & Latham, 1981). For example, did the trainees learn ways of responding to attendance-related issues? Did they acquire problem-solving principles that enabled them to deal with problems preventing them from coming to work?

To determine whether people learned and retained the knowledge disseminated in the training program, the learning test used by Frayne and Latham was administered and scored six months and nine months after the training. The coefficient alphas of the 12 situational items were .74 and .80, respectively. The trainees were not informed as to the scoring of their answers. The alpha for the replication sample calculated three months after training was .78. This compares favorably with the alpha of .82 obtained in the original three-months study. The alpha calculated for the original training group 12 months later was .84. The test-retest reliability of the questionnaire between Months 3 and 9 was .81. The test-retest reliability between the premeasure and Month 3 for the replication sample was .80. This too compares favorably with the reliability estimate of .85 obtained in the original study.

A repeated measures analysis of variance (ANOVA) revealed no significant difference among Months 3 through 9. The knowledge acquired in the training did not decrease over time. Moreover, an ANOVA revealed no significant difference between the replication sample's three-months scores and the original training group's three-months scores (Table 4.2). Thus it appears that the training led individuals to obtain knowledge on ways to overcome obstacles to coming to work.

Table 4.2
Means and Standard Deviations of Learning Measure
by Training and Control Groups

Group	Pretraining		3 Months		6 Months		9 Months		12 Months	
	M	SD	M	SD	M	SD	M	SD	M	SD
Training	15.60	4.2	29.95	7.0	28.65	6.1	28.92	10.1	27.90	8.6
Control	16.20	4.3	15.70	4.6	16.10	3.8	15.40	5.6	28.90	7.3

Note: The 12-months score is a 1-year follow-up for the training group and a 3-months follow-up for the newly trained control group.

Absenteeism and Attendance

The stability of sick leave was assessed over a 12-month period (n = 40) prior to conducting the training (Table 4.3). This was done using employee time cards. During the initial study, reliability measures were again taken at the three-month and six-month time periods (Tables 4.4 and 4.5, respectively). The test-retest reliability (stability) of the attendance measure from Month 3 until Month 12 (36 weekly measures) for the 40 employees in this study was .91, as assessed by employee time cards. This result is in sharp contrast with the stability of the sick leave categorization, namely, .39. The correlation between these two measures was − .62.

A repeated measures multivariate analysis of variance on these two dependent variables revealed a significant difference between the training and the control group on the basis of data collected in Months 3, 6, and 9, R(2,37) = 9.84, p < .05) (Tables 4.6 and 4.7). A univariate repeated measures ANOVA revealed a significant difference between the training and the control group for the attendance measure. Thus the increase in job attendance as a result of training in self-management did not diminish significantly over time. However, as was the case in the first study, the F test was only marginally significant at the .10 level for the measure of sick leave. This latter finding undoubtedly reflects its low test-retest reliability. A univariate F test for the replication sample three months subsequent to training, and for the original training group three months subsequent to training, revealed no significant differences. To understand from the employees' perspective why the training increased job attendance, employees in the original training group were assured confidentiality and were then asked to state candidly their reasons for using sick leave. This occurred during Week 2 of the training and in Months 3, 6, and 9. The procedure was not used with the replication sample because the trainer was an employee of the organization. The reasons given for sick leave are classified in Table 4.8. Of the eight reasons, family problems (e.g., "my relationship with my spouse is on the rocks, so I need to get away") were initially listed most frequently. The interviews with these individuals following the training indicated that most absences claiming to be sick leave were in fact medically related, that is, illness or a medical appointment.

COGNITIVE MEASURES

Of critical importance to this research was understanding why the training was effective from a psychological standpoint. Did training

Table 4.3
Reliability Matrix for Attendance/Absenteeism Measures
before Training

Correlation Matrix For Number of Employees Absent

Weeks	early odd	early even	mid odd	mid even	late odd
early even	.43				
mid odd	.42	.51			
mid even	.31	.43	.43		
late odd	.30	.44	.49	.32	
late even	.34	.42	.40	.36	.33

Note: N = 40, p < .05 at r = .36

Correlation Matrix for Numbers of Employees Who Come to Work

Weeks	early odd	early even	mid odd	mid even	late odd
early even	.92				
mid odd	.93	.92			
mid even	.91	.90	.93		
late odd	.87	.86	.91	.90	
late even	.93	.89	.94	.88	.87

Note: N = 40, p < .05, r = .36.

Table 4.4
Reliability Matrix for Attendance/Absenteeism
Measures at Three-Month Follow-Up

Correlation Matrix for Number of Employees Absent

Weeks	early odd	early even	mid odd	mid even	late odd
early even	.44				
mid odd	.41	.49			
mid even	.35	.47	.43		
late odd	.34	.42	.52	.32	
late even	.34	.40	.30	.35	.39

Note: N = 40, p < .05 at r = .36

Correlation Matrix for Numbers of Employees Who Come to Work

Weeks	early odd	early even	mid odd	mid even	late odd
early even	.91				
mid odd	.89	.92			
mid even	.90	.93	.92		
late odd	.84	.82	.88	.90	
late even	.92	.84	.92	.82	.84

Note: N = 40, p < .05, r = .36.

Table 4.5
Reliability Matrix for Attendance/Absenteeism
Measures at Six-Month Follow-Up

Correlation Matrix For Number of Employees Absent

Weeks	early odd	early even	mid odd	mid even	late odd
early even	.43				
mid odd	.39	.37			
mid even	.34	.47	.46		
late odd	.30	.42	.48	.34	
late even	.29	.45	.37	.36	.44

Note: N = 40, p < .05 at r = .36

Correlation Matrix for Numbers of Employees Who Come to Work

Weeks	early odd	early even	mid odd	mid even	late odd
early even	.90				
mid odd	.83	.93			
mid even	.92	.92	.92		
late odd	.91	.85	.83	.93	
late even	.85	.89	.88	.86	.85

Note: N = 40, p < .05, r = .36.

Table 4.6
Means and Standard Deviations of Attendance Measure by Training and Control Groups

Group	Pretraining		3 Months		6 Months		9 Months		12 Months	
	M	SD	M	SD	M	SD	M	SD	M	SD
Training	33.1	5.6	35.7	4.2	38.6	1.4	38.2	2.4	38.4	3.8
Control	32.3	7.6	30.0	4.9	31.6	4.3	30.9	3.3	34.9	4.3

Note: Attendance is number of hours present per 40-hr scheduled work week. The 12-months score is a 1-year follow-up for the training group and a 3-months follow-up for the newly trained control group.

Table 4.7
Means and Standard Deviations of Sick Leave Absenteeism by Training and Control Groups

Group	Pretraining		3 Months		6 Months		9 Months		12 Months	
	M	SD	M	SD	M	SD	M	SD	M	SD
Training	5.26	3.6	4.12	2.4	3.68	1.4	3.58	2.6	3.72	2.2
Control	4.96	2.2	5.03	3.6	5.14	2.8	5.11	3.9	4.01	2.4

Note: The 12-months score is a 1-year follow-up for the training group and a 3-months follow-up for the newly trained control group.

Table 4.8
Self-Reported Reasons for Absenteeism for Training Group (%)

Classification	Pretraining	3 Months	6 Months	9 Months
Family Problems	25	12	6	5
Co-Worker Problems	20	10	4	5
Transportation	15	8	5	5
Perceived Employee Privilege	12	5	5	4
Medical Appointments	10	28	30	32
Legitimate Illness	5	36	45	42
Alcohol/Drug Issues	8	-	-	-
Job Boredom	5	-	-	-

in self-management affect one's perceived self-efficacy and outcome expectancies? Do these variables predict job attendance?

Self-Efficacy

The coefficient alphas of the measure of self-efficacy for three, six, and nine months subsequent to the training of the original training group were satisfactory (.89, .89, and .97, respectively). The test-retest reliability of this measure between Months 3 and 9 was .88. In the replication sample, the alpha was .87 for the measure reported three months after the training. The test-retest reliability over three months was .89; in the original three-month study it was .92.

A repeated measures ANOVA revealed a significant difference, $F(1,119) = 27.22$, p < .01, w2 = 18, p < .05, across Months 3, 6, and 9. Perceived self-efficacy increased significantly. Moreover, an ANOVA revealed no significant difference between the original experimental and control groups three months after the training of the control group had been conducted (Table 4.9).

The correlations between self-efficacy measured three months after the training were .45, .48, and .46, respectively. All of these values were significant at the .05 level. Thus, the self-efficacy measure predicts job attendance at several points in time. A graph of this effect is shown in Figure 4.1. Self-efficacy has been found to be at the root of relapse prevention (Marlatt & Gordon, 1985).

Outcome Expectancies

The internal consistency of the outcome expectancy questionnaire at Time 1, Time 2, Time 3, and Time 4 was .67, .63, .68, and .63, respectively. The test-retest reliability between Time 1 and Time 4 was .74, between Time 2 and Time 4 was .76, and between Time 3 and Time 4 was .71.

A 2×4 repeated measures analysis of variance for the outcome expectancies measure showed no significant effects for training in self-management. The power of the test was .36, a moderately low level of power for detecting statistical significance.

Nevertheless, outcome expectancies were high initially and did not appear to change throughout this study. Past research has shown that high expected benefits do not motivate people if they have a low sense of self-efficacy (Bandura, 1982, 1986; Lee, 1984b). Although trainees' expectations in the present study were high for job attendance, prior to receiving training, these expectancies had not

Table 4.9
**Means and Standard Deviations of Self-Efficacy Measure
by Training and Control Groups**

Group	Pretraining		3 Months		6 Months		9 Months		12 Months	
	M	SD	M	SD	M	SD	M	SD	M	SD
Training	45.0	14.3	60.2	15.1	86.6	11.3	87.5	10.2	85.9	8.6
Control	46.4	13.2	45.8	14.3	46.0	12.7	44.9	13.8	63.6	12.3

Note: The 12-months score is a 1-year follow-up for the training group and a 3-months follow-up for the newly trained control group.

Figure 4.1
Self-Efficacy Scores for the Training and Control Groups

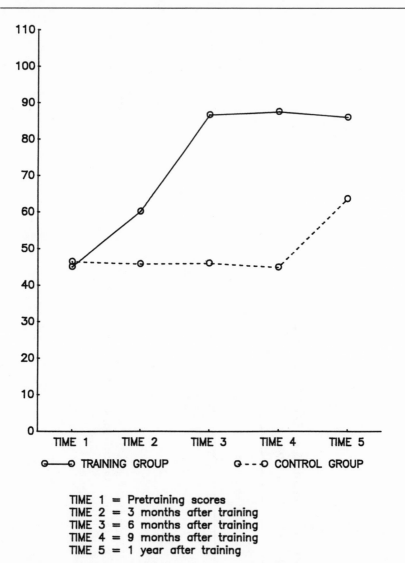

TIME 1 = Pretraining scores
TIME 2 = 3 months after training
TIME 3 = 6 months after training
TIME 4 = 9 months after training
TIME 5 = 1 year after training

Note: The 12-months score is a 1-year follow-up for the training group
and a 3-months follow-up for the newly trained control group.

influenced job attendance because perceptions of self-efficacy were low. Similarly, outcome expectancies did not change in the second study.

INTERCORRELATIONS

The intercorrelations among the variables at Times 1, 3, and 4 in the initial study are present in Table 4.10. Because the two measures of self-efficacy (i.e., strength and level) were highly correlated ($r = .93$, $p < .01$), they were combined in the analyses to provide a comprehensive measure of perceived self-efficacy. This procedure has been used previously in other studies on self-efficacy (e.g., Lichenstein & Condiotte, 1981; Godding & Glasgow, 1985; Locke et al., 1984).

Of particular importance to this study was the finding that self-efficacy correlated significantly with both job attendance and sick leave three months and again six months after the training ($r = .48$, $r = .49$, $p < .05$, Time 3 and Time 4, respectively). Outcome expectancies did not correlate with either criterion.

Finally, sick leave absenteeism and attendance were highly correlated ($r = -.67$, $r = -.64$, $r = -.65$, $p < .05$, Times 1, 3, and 4, respectively). Similar correlations were obtained in the second study.

TARDINESS AND TURNOVER

As noted in Chapter 3, neither tardiness nor turnover were viewed by the client organization as a problem. These data were collected primarily to determine whether the training program in self-management on attendance would affect these other behaviors adversely.

There were no significant differences in either tardiness or turnover between the training and control groups throughout the entire study, $X = 2.8\%$ and $X = 4\%$, respectively. This finding is important in that previous writers on absenteeism have warned against using a symptom-oriented strategy when encouraging individuals to come to work. For example, Rosse and Miller (1984) have argued that absenteeism may represent one of the many possible symptoms of dissatisfaction with one's work role. A treatment program aimed at only one of many possible responses to job dissatisfaction or commitment may result in "symptom substitution" wherein declining absence is accompanied by increased tardiness or turnover.

Table 4.10
Intercorrelations[a] of All Variables[b]

Before Training:[c]

Variable	(1)	(2)	(3)	(4)	(5)	(6)
(1) Learning	-	.31	.18	.41	.35	.03
(2) Self-Efficacy		-	.28	.23	.29	.40
(3) Outcome Expectancy			-	.31	.18	.15
(4) Attendance				-	.67	.23
(5) Sick Leave					-	.18
(6) Tardiness						-

3 Months After Training:[c]

Variable	(1)	(2)	(3)	(4)	(5)	(6)
(1) Reaction	-	.41	.35	.21	.48	.35
(2) Learning		-	.43	.37	.35	.36
(3) Self-Efficacy			-	.31	.49	.40
(4) Outcome Expectancy				-	.26	.23
(5) Attendance					-	.65
(6) Sick Leave						-

Six Months After Training:[c]

Variable	(1)	(2)	(3)	(4)	(5)	(6)
(1) Reaction	-	.42	.34	.24	.42	.39
(2) Learning		-	.31	.36	.39	.31
(3) Self-efficacy			-	.33	.48	.43
(4) Outcome Expectancy				-	.29	.19
(5) Attendance					-	.64
(6) Sick Leave						-

[a]: Decimal points were dropped for all correlations.

[b]: $N = 40$, $r > .36$, significant at $p < .05$.

[c]: Only dependent measures relevant at each respective time interval appear in the matrix.

SIGNIFICANCE OF THE RESEARCH STUDIES

The results of both studies suggest that self-management training based on social learning theory can be effective in increasing employee attendance. The employees who received training in self-management (1) felt the training was useful for them, (2) learned how to overcome obstacles preventing them from coming to work, (3) increased their feelings of self-efficacy, and (4) most important, increased their attendance on the job. This chapter discusses these findings in the light of their theoretical and practical significance, the limitations of the data, the advantages and limitations of self-management, and some suggested directions for future research.

Theoretical Significance

The theoretical significance of these studies is that they provide an explanation of why people choose to come to work or not to come to work. The results of the studies suggest that people who come to work may be individuals who are able to overcome the personal obstacles and the cultural and group norms identified by Chadwick-Jones and colleagues (1982) as affecting a person's perceived ability to come to work. People who do not come to work may be unable to cope with these influences unless their self-efficacy is enhanced by providing them with skills for exercising control over these influences. The key psychological variable affecting behavior change appears to be self-efficacy. Thus absenteeism may no longer be a social fact in need of a theory: self-efficacy is one such theory (Bandura, 1982).

Of further theoretical significance is the finding that high outcome expectancies alone will not result in employees coming to work if they judge themselves as unable to overcome personal and social obstacles to work attendance. This finding is in accord with other studies that showed that a sense of low self-efficacy counteracts the motivation of outcome expectancies (Barling & Abel, 1983; Godding & Glasgow, 1985; Lee, 1984b).

Practical Significance

The practical significance of these studies is eightfold. First, they showed the external validity of training in self-management for unionized workers employed by a state government. Until the present series, training in self-management had been restricted primarily to people in clinical or educational settings.

Second, these studies showed the effectiveness of training in self-management in an area that had not been previously studied using this technique, namely, employee attendance. Employee attendance, as noted in Chapter 1, has significant cost implications for organizations.

Third, the rival hypothesis that the effects of the training were trainer-specific was rejected. Of special importance with regard to application was that the trainding in the replication study was conducted by a layperson in the organization's personnel department.

Fourth, employee attendance at work increased on the basis of a straightforward 12-hour training program. While elements of the program—goal setting, reinforcers—are not new, what is unique is the emphasis on trainees developing a contract with themselves for self-administering reinforcers and punishers to facilitate goal commitment.

Fifth, the effectiveness of this training does not appear to diminish with time. Reaction, learning, self-efficacy, and job attendance measures taken nine months after the training showed that training in self-management brings about a relatively permanent change in cognition, affect, and behavior.

Sixth, the studies provided a stringent test of training in self-management. Both groups, after all, wanted to change behavior, to increase attendance at work; both attended the orientation session (recall that people were randomly assigned to either the experimental or the control group). Thus it is apparent that the behavior changes in the trained group were due specifically to the effects of their training—and not to such factors as evaluation apprehension or attention.

Seventh, there appears to be no evidence of symptom substitution on the part of those who practice self-management techniques. This fact, plus the cost effectiveness of this training, casts significant doubt on the assertion of Nicholson and his colleagues (e.g., Chadwick-Jones, Nicholson, & Brown, 1982) that the utility of behavioral interventions that focus on the individual are of questionable value.

Eighth, the studies showed the importance of using attendance rather than a measure of absenteeism as the primary dependent variable. This point has been argued elsewhere (Latham & Napier, 1984; Latham & Frayne, 1986), but the superiority of the former measure for assessing the effects of an intervention had not been demonstrated empirically. Measures of absenteeism are typically nothing more than measures of the categorization behavior of recorders (Latham & Pursell, 1975, 1977). They often reflect the outcome of negotiated behavior between a superior and a subordinate. That is, an absence is sometimes classified as sick leave rather than as a vacation day as a reward for good performance (Goodman & Atkin, 1984). Thus absenteeism measures are highly contaminated (Thorndike, 1949), and their reliability is typically quite low. If a measure of recorded sick leave had been used in this study as the sole index of absenteeism, a Type II error would have been made. The results would have shown that training in self-management had only a marginal effect on employee absenteeism.

LIMITATIONS OF THE RESEARCH STUDIES

The limitations in the studies discussed are threefold. First, as noted in Chapter 3, both attendance and absenteeism measures ignored the distinction between volunatry and involuntary absenteeism. Some people may have taken sick leave because they were in fact too ill to come to work, while others may have persuaded their supervisors to record what should have been a vacation day as a sick leave day. These two behaviors, illness and persuasion, are obviously very different. To overcome this problem in future studies of absenteeism, investigators who wish to study absenteeism in isolation must observe people while they stay away from work. The reliability of such observers will of course be a factor to be reckoned with.

Second, the cultural and normative effects of absenteeism were not empirically examined. If trainee self-efficacy had not increased in this study, the role of cultural and normative factors might have served in a later study as useful moderator variables to explain the results. The present studies, however, do suggest that self-regulatory techniques, based on social learning theory, can be used to overcome inhibiting normative behaviors. In fact, the very essence of training in self-management is teaching the individual how to overcome or resist such norms. Blaming either society or the informal absenteeism norms of an organization for one's poor attendance record is unlikely to prevent the person from being fired.

Anecdotal evidence supported the assertion that training in self-management enables people to cope effectively with group norms. Trainees reported that they often ate lunch together and discussed their dissatisfaction with poor supervision and unfavorable working conditions and their disillusionment within individual units of the organization. Six trainees reported that this type of socializing led to a "poor attitude" on their part and a subsequent feeling of helplessness. Two reported that they would use a few hours of sick leave to leave work early to relieve stress experienced in these situations.

Once the trainees had identified this problem during the self-assessment session, each individual set goals aimed at managing the stressful effects. For example, two of the trainees decided to eat lunch elsewhere. In addition, they devised a number of alternative places to take their allotted breaks during the workday. After the training, these two individuals credited these alternative actions and problem-solving strategies as instrumental to their overcoming feelings of stress and subsequently increasing their job attendance.

Third, whether the findings can be generalized to subjects who do not volunteer for a training program may need to be assessed. Yet the verbal and physical assaults that took place initially among the trainees raise questions as to whether the training was in fact perceived by the trainees as voluntary.

FUTURE RESEARCH

The findings of the studies presented in this book provide several directions for future research. First, the application of self-management training to other workplace problem behaviors (for example, learned helplessness, alcoholism, drug abuse, ineffective job performance) involving middle and upper managers in different organizational settings would appear warranted.

The powerful effect of self-efficacy on employee attendance suggests that an individual's overall performance may be increased by enhancing self-efficacy. Self-efficacy may indeed affect the full range of a person's level of self-esteem and/or locus of control. Future research should examine this possibility.

Finally, outcome expectancies are usually measured in terms of external rewards and punishers. But social learning theory also emphasizes the impact of internal standards or goals on self-regulation. When a person's performance falls short of a goal, he or she is dissatisfied and motivated to increased effort (Bandura, 1986; Bandura & Cervone, 1983). Thus self-motivation is regulated by both self-efficacy and self-evaluation. It would be informative in future research to measure self-evaluative outcomes as well as anticipated external ones.

SUMMARY

The theoretical significance of these studies is that they provide an explanation of why people choose to come or not to come to work. The practical significance is eightfold.

1. They show the external validity of training in self-management for a broader segment of society—not only, as earlier, to people in clinical or educational settings.
2. They treat an area not previously studied—employee attendance.
3. They dispel the hypothesis that training effects are training-specific.
4. They demonstrate, simply, that the training works—employee attendance increased as a result of the 12-hour training program.
5. They indicate that the training's effectiveness does not diminish with time.
6. They show that the behavior changes in the trained group were due specifically to the effects of the training itself, not to such factors as evaluation apprehension or attention.
7. They underscore the utility of behavioral interventions that focus on the individual.
8. They attest to the importance of using attendance rather than absenteeism as the primary dependent variable.

5

HOW TO USE SELF-MANAGEMENT EFFECTIVELY

INTRODUCTION

The previous chapters have demonstrated the use of self-management training for reducing absenteeism. Critical to these robust results is the effective implementation of the training program, a topic to which this chapter devotes itself.

Self-management is generally introduced through training individuals in the basic techniques and then measuring their performance over time. The training program is straightforward, flexible, and easily adaptable to fit the individual's job demands and schedule. Below are specific strategies and procedures for developing self-management behavior in employees in the sequence in which they should be practiced and implemented.

SELF-ASSESSMENT

Self-assessment provides the foundation for self-management. This technique involves systematic data gathering about one's own behavior. The aim is to identify when, why, and under what conditions the person behaves in certain ways and achieves certain levels of performance. For example, a manager who believes that he or she is unable to address longer-term strategic issues adequately because of too many interruptions during the workday should study the distractions. Am I spending too much time in informal conversations? Am I constantly being interrupted by telephone calls? Am I fighting fires that my subordinates should be attending to instead?

By observing the amount of time spent on repetitive administrative tasks or informal conversations, for example, the individual can learn more about this behavior. The individual should record the type and number of such conversations in each workday and the conditions that existed at the time. If three hours are spent chatting informally during an eight-hour day, it becomes a bit more clear as to why the performance goals are not being accomplished. Furthermore, if most of the individual's conversations begin at the coffee room, the person has useful information for managing the behavior, for example, by cutting down on trips to the coffee lounge. Pinpointing the interruptions as specifically as possible can help the manager or employee decide which interruptions are the most troublesome and which should be targeted for modification through self-management.

In the studies under discussion, the trainees were asked during the orientation session why they had volunteered for training. As noted earlier, their responses fell into one or more of the following categories:

1. Dissatisfaction with current policies regarding absenteeism (policies viewed as punitive)
2. Acknowledgment of problems with job attendance
3. An interest in learning self-management skills to deal not only with job attendance but also with other problem behaviors such as excessive smoking and gaining weight

The trainer explained the underlying assumptions and rationale of self-management and took measures of self-efficacy and outcome expectancies (to be taken again immediately after, three months after, six months after, and nine months after the training). A learning test was also administered during this session (and again at three months, six months, and nine months following training).

In Week 2 of the research, the trainer classified the reasons given previously for using sick leave into eight categories as follows:

1. Family problems
2. Supervisor or coworker problems
3. Transportation difficulties
4. Sick leave seen as a right, privilege
5. Medical appointments
6. Legitimate illness
7. Alcohol and drug-related issues
8. Job boredom

Of these eight reasons, family problems (for example, "my spouse doesn't have sick leave, so when the children are sick, I stay home," "my relationship with my spouse is on the rocks and I need to get away"), incompatibility with supervisors or coworkers (for example, "my supervisor never listens to my problems"), and transportation problems (for example, "my car breaks down," "I miss my ride," "I refuse to use the bus") were listed most frequently. Table 5.1 shows the categories and corresponding response frequencies measured during this session. These measures were collected again during the follow-up periods at three, six, and nine months during the initial study. Similar results were obtained during the second study.

Table 5.1
Self-Reported Reasons for Absenteeism

Classification	Session 2
Family Problems	25%
Co-Worker Problems	20%
Transportation	15%
Privilege	12%
Medical Appointments	10%
Legitimate Illness	5%
Alcohol/Drug Issues	8%
Job Boredom	5%

These categories of response strongly support the findings of Goodman and Atkin (1984) in their research with coal miners—people who take sick leave frequently are not sick.

During the self-assessment portion of the course, each trainee was taught to

1. identify and define what self-assessment means (Figure 5.1)
2. develop a description of specific problem behaviors
3. identify those conditions that elicit and maintain inappropriate behaviors and record them on the form provided (Figures 5.2 and 5.3)
4. identify the specific behaviors desired

For example, where "supervisory difficulty" was reported as a problem, the trainees learned to define the term objectively, giving specific examples of actual occurrences and their consequences. A case study (Figure 5.4) provided opportunities for practicing these skills at a distance before turning to their own personal situations. The trainer helped the trainees to focus both on their own responses and on the actions taken by their respective supervisors (or coworkers if the problem lay with them). The trainees recorded their responses on self-assessment forms (Figure 5.5), thus clarifying for themselves the problem or problems that they wanted to overcome in order to increase job attendance.

GOAL SETTING

After determining which behaviors need to be changed, it is essential that the individual develop self-established goals. Goals provide direction for an employee's efforts that might otherwise be characterized by sporadic, reactionary activity with no consistent, purposeful basis. This technique also allows the individual to set both short-term and long-term goals for improving performance. For example, the manager who discovers that three hours per day are spent in informal conversations might set a long-term goal of limiting these conversations to one hour per day and an immediate goal of reducing them to two hours per day. Similarly, the individual who is spending too much time on the telephone might set a specific goal to complete X projects per day and hold and/or screen all incoming phone calls until half or all of the projects have been completed. Goal setting is more effective if the goals are specific, challenging, and

Figure 5.1
Self-Assessment Principles

1. Self-assessment involves specifying the problem in terms of your behavior in particular situations.

2. Behavior is affected by its antecedents (situations that come before the behavior) and by its consequences (situations that come after the behavior). Each person, however, through thoughts and feelings, interprets each situation differently.

3. The behavior chosen to modify or change is called the target behavior.

4. The behavior specified must be observable, countable, and specific.

5. The objective of self-assessment is to pinpoint and break down the behavior in particular situations in which it occurs in order to determine what will be worked on.

Source: Adapted from *Self-Directed Behavior: Self-Modification for Personal Adjustment,* fourth edition, by D. L. Watson and R. G. Tharp. Copyright 1984 by Wadsworth, Inc. Reprinted by permission of the publisher, Brooks/Cole Publishing Company, Pacific Grove, California.

Figure 5.2
Self-Assessment Tactics

A. Tactics for Specifying Behavior-in-Situations:
   1. Make a list of concrete examples.
   2. Look for examples in your daily life.
   3. Ask yourself what you would be doing if you were at your goal.
   4. Observe your behavior in various situations.

B. Sometimes you want to CHANGE a behavior, to begin something YOU ARE NOT doing now. To determine what behavior you should change:
   1. See what you are doing in the target situation. Are you doing something incompatible with your target behavior? You should specify not only the situation and the fact that the desirable behavior is not occurring, but also the behaviors that do occur instead of the ones you want.
   2. See what you should be doing in the target situation. What desirable behaviors can you increase? You should specify the situations in which you want the behavior to occur.

Figure 5.2 (continued)

3. Specify the chain of actions that you feel will produce the target behavior.

4. Watch someone who does attain your target behavior, and see what he or she is doing.

Source: Adapted from *Self-Directed Behavior: Self-Modification for Personal Adjustment,* fourth edition, by D. L. Watson and R. G. Tharp. Copyright 1984 by Wadsworth, Inc. Reprinted by permission of the publisher, Brooks/Cole Publishing Company, Pacific Grove, California.

Figure 5.3
Self-Assessment Worksheet

A. BEHAVIOR	FREQUENCY	WHEN (day/mo)	WHY
1.			
2.			
3.			
4.			
5.			

B. ANTECEDENTS	BEHAVIORS	CONSEQUENCES

Source: Adapted from *The Art of Self-Leadership*, by C. C. Manz. Copyright 1983. Prentice-Hall.

Figure 5.4
Self-Assessment Case Study

Fred Smith is an employee of the Physical Plant Services of ABC University. He has been employed in the machine shop department for five years and is recently being considered for a promotion to shop foreman.

During the last six months, Fred has been missing at least one day each week, and his absence is becoming noticeable and bothersome to some of the other employees who must do his work in addition to completing their own responsibilities.

Fred knows that he needs to specify what problems he is having that prevent him from coming to work. You are Fred's best buddy at work and feel you should discuss the problem with him. You are currently enrolled in a self-management training course and feel you might be able to share some of your ideas and techniques you learned in the class with Fred. How can you help Fred?
Specifically:

1. What can he do to identify his problems with job attendance? What questions should he be asking himself?

2. Use examples in your daily life as possible problems that he may be encountering and list ways to solve them.

3. What methods do you recommend that he use?

4. What does your self-assessment analysis look like? Put it in an outline form and be prepared to discuss it with your fellow trainees.

difficult, yet attainable. If an individual sets unreasonable goals that cannot be achieved realistically—for example, reducing informal conversations to 15 minutes per day, immediately—the outcome is likely to cause more harm than good.

In Week 3 of the studies under discussion, the employees were taught to set specific, difficult but attainable goals for obtaining the target behavior (i.e., increasing attendance on the job) they had identified during the self-assessment session. The proximal goals were directly related to the employees' desired changes regarding perceived obstacles (e.g., "I will spend two hours each day with my spouse"). Thus the goals consisted of observable, discrete, countable behaviors identified by the trainees.

The distal goal was to increase attendance within a specific time frame (e.g., at the end of each month, at the end of three months).

Figure 5.5
Self-Assessment Form

___

As a result of today's session:

1.   I'd like to exert more self control over the following area of my
     behavior:

     _____

     _____.

2.   I'd like to increase or decrease the following specific behavior:

           INCREASE   DECREASE

     1.   1.

     2.   2.

     3.   3.

3.   Can the behavior be measured as it is currently described? If
     not, restate the behavior so that it is countable.

     _____

     _____.

4.   I estimate that the behavior currently occurs at the level of (#
     of times).

     _____ per week   _____ per year

     _____ per month

Source: Adapted from "Self-Management Procedures," by F. Andrasik and J.
            Heimberg, 1982. In L. W. Frederiksen (ed.), *Handbook of Organizational
            Behavior Management*. Copyright © 1982 by John Wiley & Sons, Inc.
            Reprinted by permission of John Wiley & Sons, Inc.

Tactics for specifying their goals (Figure 5.6) were explained to all
trainees. A measure of goal commitment was taken immediately after
the eighth training session (see Figure 3.5).

A case study (Figure 5.7) and several important learning principles
of goal setting (Figure 5.8) were introduced and used as practice tools
for training the individuals in goal-setting procedures. The goal-
setting worksheet (Figure 5.9) was used to record the trainees' goals
and means of achieving those goals.

Figure 5.6
Goal-Setting Tactics

A. Tactics for Specifying Goals
  1. Ask yourself what you would be doing if you were at your goal.
  2. Phrase the goal as behaviors in situations. Ask yourself, under which circumstances do I want to do which behaviors?
  3. The goal should include both the behavior to be changed and the situations in which it will change. The diagram below will help you to identify the specific situation that occurs, the resulting behavior, and what goal(s) you will set as a result of the behavior that occurs.

  SITUATION   BEHAVIOR   GOAL SET

B. Identify all behaviors that contribute to the problem interfering with your attaining your goals.
  1. Ask yourself, what am I doing that interferes with my goal?
  2. What behaviors do I have to perform to reach it?
  3. It may be helpful to observe the behavior of other people achieving similar goals to yours and see how they are doing it.
  4. What are your overall (long-range) goals for attendance? What subgoals (short-range—weekly, monthly) will you set?

  Your goals for attendance are critical to your success in changing your behavior

Source: Adapted from *Self-Directed Behavior: Self-Modification for Personal Adjustment,* fourth edition, by D. L. Watson and R. G. Tharp. Copyright 1984 by Wadsworth, Inc. Reprinted by permission of the publisher, Brooks/Cole Publishing Company, Pacific Grove California.

SELF-MONITORING

Self-monitoring, which is a precondition for self-evaluation, is the process by which an individual maintains a record of progress toward goal attainment and examines ways in which the environment is hindering the attainment of these goals. The behavior to be monitored, identified during the goal-setting session—for example, the number of informal conversations during the work day—would

Figure 5.7
Goal-Setting Case Study

Last week, you applied a self-assessment technique to analyze Fred Smith's problem at the workplace. You identified the following:

1. The specific problem behaviors that were keeping him from coming to work each day

2. What events occurred immediately before his decision to stay home from work

3. What the consequences of this decision were

4. The feelings, thoughts, and behaviors that he experienced as a result of being absent from work

In this training session, you learned that goals should be set once the individual has correctly and specifically identified the behavior(s) that he or she wants to change or increase. Again, putting yourself in Fred's role:

1. How would you go about setting goals for this situation? Each group should take one problem that was identified from the self-assessment session (for example, difficulty with supervisor, family problems, transportation difficulties) and set goals based on that problem behavior, only.

2. What goals would you set?

3. What criteria would you use to assess these goals?

4. In your list of goals, which ones are short-range? Long-range?

5. How will you assess your progress regarding goal accomplishment?

Figure 5.8
Goal-Setting Principles

1. Goals are standards by which one can measure performance.

2. The goals that are set must be specific.

3. Goals should be both proximal (short-range) and distal (long-range) in nature.

4. The goals set by the individual must be acceptable, challenging, yet attainable. Goal commitment is critical to self-management application.

5. The goals provide the individual with a benchmark or standard with which to compare actual performance.

Figure 5.9
Goal-Setting Worksheet

GOAL SET   WHEN PERFORMED   HOW   PROGRESS REVIEW

Examine the chart you filled in above. Answer the following questions
below about the goals you specified:

1.   Can the behavior be measured as it is currently described? If
     not, restate the behavior so that it is countable.

---

2.   I would like to increase the:

     (a) frequency of   _____.

     (b) duration of   _____.

     (c) amount of   _____.

     (d) quality of   _____.

3.   I would like the behavior to occur at the level of:

     _____ per week   _____ per month

     _____ per year

4.   My goals for increasing my attendance are:

Source: Adapted from "Self-Management Procedures," by F. Andrasik and J.
            Heimberg, 1982. In L. W. Frederiksen (ed.), *Handbook of Organizational
            Behavior Management*. Copyright © 1982 by John Wiley & Sons, Inc.
            Reprinted by permission of John Wiley & Sons, Inc.

85

be used by the individual to determine what self-monitoring system would be employed.

To be effective, the monitoring system chosen must be simple and must fit into the individual's daily routine. For example, the manager wishing to reduce the number of informal telephone calls might keep a notepad next to the phone to record the number, type, and length of discussions each day and use this as a standard to compare against a self-set goal.

It is important that the individual record the behavior in a timely, accurate manner, such as daily or weekly, and as close in time to the occurrence of the behavior as possible. Examples of measurement tools that can be used by self-managers include wall graphs, charts, diaries, performance reports, and timing devices. Although it may appear time-consuming to a busy individual, self-monitoring of one's progress toward goals is critical, since goal setting in the absence of self-monitoring has no effect whatsoever on changing behavior.

During the fourth week of the training session in the studies under review, each employee was taught what to monitor, how to monitor, and when to record the behaviors to be performed (Figures 5.10 and 5.11). The individuals used the behaviors to be monitored that had been identified during the self-observation session (e.g., steps to overcoming an obstacle, frequency of attendance behavior) to determine what self-monitoring system would be employed. The self-monitoring measurement device questionnaire (Figure 5.12) helped the trainees determine what methods would be appropriate and convenient for them to use.

The need to record behavior in a timely, accurate manner was emphasized (i.e., each day, as close as possible in time to the occurrence of the behavior). Finally, instruction was given on the use of various measurement instruments (e.g., wall graphs, charts, diaries). Each trainee selected a method that was simple, portable, and easy to use. Figure 5.13 shows an example of a trainee's attendance chart.

A case study scenario (Figure 5.14) requiring effective self-monitoring practices was used during the session to give the trainees an opportunity to practice self-monitoring techniques before implementing them into their own programs.

SELF-EVALUATION

Self-evaluation, which leads to the use of self-reinforcement and/or self-punishment strategies, is a powerful method for

Figure 5.10
Self-Monitoring Principles

1. Self-monitoring involves keeping records of the specific behavior targeted for change as well as the antecedent events and the consequences of the behavior.
2. The behavior should be counted and recorded as soon as it occurs.
3. The individual must be accurate and strict in counting the desired behavior.
4. The recording device and system must be simple, portable, and easy to use.
5. Written records as well as graphs of the behavior should be kept.
6. The objective of self-monitoring is to observe, record, and evaluate your own behavior over a period of time.

Figure 5.11
Self-Monitoring Guidelines

1. You should do the counting as the events occur. When making a simple count, record the situation in which the absence occurs.
2. Keep your system to record the behavior simple, easy to use.
3. You must be strict in your counting; always keep written records of your behavior.
4. The idea behind self-monitoring is to build record-keeping into your pattern of habitual behaviors. You may reward yourself initially for keeping records for attendance and then switch over to just rewarding yourself for good attendance.
5. As soon as you realize you have performed some undesired target behavior or failed to perform some desired one, make an entry in your log. You should describe the physical setting, the social situation, your thoughts, and the behavior of the other people, if appropriate.
6. Try to record entries as soon as the target behavior occurs or fails to occur. The main reasons for this approach are to get a better understanding of the behavior that is occurring and also to develop a standard by which to evaluate your progress over time.
7. When self-monitoring, the following tactics may serve as reminders:
    a) Use *specifically* defined categories.
    b) The *behavior and situation* should be recorded on a

Figure 5.11 (continued)

   c) *device* always present with a

   d) *simple system* that is

   e) *NOT* difficult to use.

Source: Adapted from *Self-Directed Behavior: Self-Modification for Personal Adjustment,* fourth edition, by D. L. Watson and R. G. Tharp. Copyright 1984 by Wadsworth, Inc. Reprinted by permission of the publisher, Brooks/Cole Publishing Company, Pacific Grove, California.

enhancing self-management effectiveness. The individual examines his or her performance against the goals that were set. Either reinforcers or punishers are then used, depending upon the degree to which the behavior diverges from the performance goals.

Self-reinforcement involves the self-delivery of pleasant consequences after the achievement of a goal. By providing rewards for achieving self-set goals, a positive influence on future actions can be exerted. An expensive dinner at your favorite restaurant, a new suit, or an evening free of work are examples of rewards that can be self-administered. The rewards need not be tangible, however. They may consist of simply "a pat on the back" or telling oneself, "I did a heck of a job," when the self-monitoring activity reveals that, for example, the goal of one hour of informal conversations per day has been achieved.

Self-punishment, which attempts to reduce undesired behavior by self-administering aversive consequences, does not seem to exhibit the same high level of effectiveness as a self-reinforcement. Successful use of self-punishment requires the consequence to be sufficiently powerful to affect the undesired behavior, yet not so aversive that it will not be used. For the individual who has not achieved the weekly goal of reducing informal conversations, requiring that he or she devote the evening to completing work at home rather than going out with friends might be more useful than requiring the person to relinquish a week of holiday time. Similarly, mentally telling oneself, "I did a lousy job," may be an effective, nontangible form of self-punishment that encourages the individual to continue trying to meet the goals without causing total abandonment. If the individual continually fails to meet the self-set goal, it is time to re-examine the

Figure 5.12
Self-Monitoring Measurement Device

A. Questions to aid you in designing an individualized system of
    measurement:

    1. I think the best way for me to assess my current level of
        behavior and any progress I make would be to count its
        frequency, duration, or amount every:

        _____ hour   _____ week

        _____ month   _____ other

    2. Can the behavior be counted immediately or almost immediately
        after it occurs? _____ If not, what is the most
        immediate way of noting that the behavior has occurred?

        _____

    3. How many persons can possibly observe the behavior?
        self _____   family member _____
        co-worker _____   supervisor _____
        other _____

    4. Who will record the behavior?

    5. What arrangements must be made to establish your behavior
        recording system? (e.g., checklist inside locker door?
        notepad in your pocket?)

Source: Adapted from "Self-Management Procedures," by F. Andrasik and J.
           Heimberg, 1982. In L. W. Frederiksen (ed.), *Handbook of Organizational
           Behavior Management*. Copyright © 1982 by John Wiley & Sons, Inc.
           Reprinted by permission of John Wiley & Sons, Inc.

Figure 5.13
Trainee's Attendance Chart

WEEK	M	T	W	TH	F
9/23	8	8	8	8	8
9/30	8	8	8	8	8
10/7	8	8	8	8	8
10/14	8	8	5 (doctor appointment)	8	8
10/21	8	8	8	8	8
10/28	0 (outpatient surgery)	0 (recovery)	8	8	8
11/4	8	8	8	6 (follow-up appointment)	8
11/11	8	8	8	8	8
11/18	8	8	8	8	8
11/25	8	8	8	8	8
12/2	8	8	8	8	8
12/9	6	8	8	8	8
12/16	8	8	8	8	8
12/23	8	HOLIDAY	8	8	8
12/30	8	HOLIDAY	8	8	8
1/6	8	8	8	8	8
1/13	8	8	8	8	8
1/20	8	7 (argument with boss)	0 (asthma attack)	8	8
1/27	8	8	8	8	8
2/3	8	8	8	8	8
2/10	8	8	8	8	8
2/17	8	8	8	8	8
2/24	8	8	8	6 (doctor appointment)	8
3/3	8	8	8	8	8

Figure 5.14
Self-Monitoring Case Study

During the last training session, you applied a goal-setting technique to identify a set of new behaviors and performance standards that Fred would strive to attain in order to increase his attendance on the job. These goals were based on the problem behaviors pinpointed during the self-assessment session. The specific behaviors you assessed concerned (1) interpersonal problems with supervisors, (2) family problems, (3) transportation difficulties, and (4) legitimate illness.

This week, you learned that self-monitoring is a way to record the behaviors that you want to increase and to assess your progression toward your self-set goals. Again, place yourself in Fred's role and take a look at the goals you have set.

1. What behaviors are you going to self-monitor?

2. How are you going to monitor them? What devices or tools will you use? A notebook? Chart? Diary? How often are you going to monitor the behaviors?

3. When will you monitor the behavior? Under what circumstances will the recording of the behavior occur? At work? Privately? At home?

4. Will there be any one else monitoring the behavior as well? A friend? Your supervisor? Will you use any self-reminders?

5. Give an example of a graph or chart that Fred could use to monitor his attendance behavior.

---

commitment to the goal, the realistic attainability of the goal, and/or the self-monitoring system used to track goal attainment.

In the fifth week of both studies, the principles of self-reinforcement and self-punishment were introduced (Figure 5.15). Next, the trainees identified reinforcers and punishers to self-administer as a result of achieving or failing to achieve their proximal goals (Figure 5.16). In identifying the reinforcers and punishers, two considerations were emphasized. First, the consequence had to be a strong reinforcer for the individual; second, the reinforcer had to be easily self-administered. Questions for selecting reinforcers were provided to aid the trainee (Figure 5.17). With regard to punishers, the individual was taught to administer one from a self-generated list of disliked activities (e.g., picking up after everyone in the family for one day, cleaning the garage). Each individual developed specific response

Figure 5.15
Self-Evaluation Principles

1. You should determine the reward most appropriate for yourself in terms of availability and importance.
2. The reinforcers or punishers should be applied soon after the occurrence of the desired or the undesired behavior.
3. The methods used to reinforce and punish must be clear, acceptable, and available in the situations you have specified.
4. Use a variety of reinforcers to avoid satiation from one specific type.

Figure 5.16
Self-Evaluation Guidelines

A. Effects of Consequences
   1. If a consequence strengthens behavior, it is called a REINFORCER.
   2. A positive reinforcer is a consequence that strengthens behavior by its added presence.
   3. A behavior that is punished will occur less often. There are two types of punishment: (1) addition of an unpleasant consequence, and (2) withdrawal of a pleasant consequence.
   4. Examples of positive reinforcers are food, money, and praise. Reinforcers are highly individualized, and what is important and works for one person may not work for another.
   5. Examples of punishers are a reprimand from your supervisor, disapproval from a friend, and loss of a privilege for abuse of it. If the punisher is powerful enough, the behavior that led to that event is less likely to happen in the future.

B. Basic Techniques for Reinforcement
   1. You can select any reinforcer that you wish and make it contingent on the target behavior.
   2. You must be sure that the reinforcer you select is potent, accessible, and manipulatable.
   3. The sooner the reinforcer occurs after the target behavior, the more it reinforces the behavior.
   4. When choosing the reinforcers, keep the following in mind:
      a) The reinforcer must be accessible to you.
      b) Choose potent reinforcers.
      c) Try to reinforce the behavior quickly after performing it.

Figure 5.16 (continued)

5. Problems to avoid in reinforcement include:
   a) Do not overuse the reinforcer. Select several different ones.
   b) If there is more than one behavior to change, use a separate reinforcer for each.
   c) Use activities as reinforcers (taking yourself out to dinner or to a movie).

Figure 5.17
Self-Evaluation Questionnaire

Questions for Selecting a Reinforcer:

1. What will be the rewards of achieving your goal?
2. What kind of praise do you like to receive—from yourself, or from others?
3. What kinds of things do you like to have?
4. What are your major interests?
5. What are your hobbies?
6. What people do you like to be with?
7. What do you like to do with those people?
8. What do you do for fun?
9. What do you do to relax?
10. What do you do to get away from it all?
11. What would be a nice present to receive?
12. What kinds of things are important to you?
13. What behaviors do you perform every day?
14. Are there any behaviors that you usually engage in instead of the target behavior?
15. What would you hate to lose?
16. Of the things you do every day, what would you hate to give up?

Source: Adapted from *Self-Directed Behavior: Self-Modification for Personal Adjustment,* fourth edition, by D. L. Watson and R. G. Tharp. Copyright 1984 by Wadsworth, Inc. Reprinted by permission of the publisher, Brooks/Cole Publishing Company, Pacific Grove, California.

reinforcement or punishment contingencies that specified the precise conditions and methods for delivering the consequences (e.g., "I will reward myself each Friday night with an ice cream cone for each week that I have a perfect attendance record"). These responses were recorded on worksheets provided during the training session (Figure 5.18).

The case study (Figure 5.19) for this section of the course related to self-reward and self-punishment strategies, enabling the trainees to put these strategies into practice.

WRITTEN CONTRACTS

Written contracts are another integral part of self-management training. A contract is a written agreement with oneself that specifies expectations, plans, and contingencies for the behavior to be

Figure 5.18
Self-Evaluation Worksheet

After you have identified reinforcers and punishers, you can enter these into the following chart:

BEHAVIOR(S)   REWARD USED   RESULTS

UNDESIRABLE BEHAVIOR(S)   STRATEGY USED   RESULTS

Source: Adapted from *The Art of Self-Leadership,* by C. C. Manz. Copyright 1983. Prentice-Hall.

Figure 5.19
Self-Evaluation Case Study

Last week, you identified strategies for monitoring Fred Smith's behaviors that he is trying to change and/or increase. A device or system of measurement was chosen to keep a record of each time Fred performed the behavior and under what circumstances. Some of the systems recommended for measuring attendance included wall charts, calendars, and graphs.

In order to maintain his desired level of performance, you learned that giving him rewards for meeting self-set goals and administering punishers for not meeting his goals is an important technique for self-managing behavior. Based on the goals he has set, how would you establish rewards and punishers to ensure that the new behavior(s) is(are) made a permanent part of Fred's present behavior?
Specifically:

1. What reinforcers are you going to use? How will you generate them?
2. What punishers are you going to use? How will you generate them?
3. When will you use them to reinforce or punish the behavior? How often?
4. What criteria will you use to check that you are generating the reinforcers and punishers correctly?

---

changed. The purpose of the contract is to specify (1) the goals that are set, (2) the actions that the person will take to attain the goals, and (3) the contingencies for self-administering the rewards or punishers (Figure 5.20). The contract is actually an antecedent to administering the self-management program; it will prompt the individual to follow through on the planned course of action and also serve as another form of goal commitment. Contracts for self-management programs are basically contracts with oneself, although the participation of another person such as a supervisor or a coworker may improve the contract's effectiveness.

During the sixth week of training, each employee wrote a formal plan that specified (1) the goals to be achieved, (2) the method of monitoring goal attainment, (3) the self-generated consequences for achieving or failing to achieve one's goals, and (4) methods for achieving the desired change in behavior (Figure 5.21). An example of a trainee's behavioral contract is shown in Figure 5.22.

As in the other sessions of the course, the case study (Figure 5.23) in this instance was specifically tied to the subject matter: behavioral contracts. In regard to making their own contracts, the trainees learned about the features of a good contract and steps to use when

Figure 5.20
Written Contract Principles

---

1. A contract is an agreement about the nature and conduct of the individual's responsibilities during the self-management training.

2. A contract should be formulated for a specific time frame.

3. The contract must be used systematically.

4. Of central importance to the individual establishing the contract is that he or she understands the terms of the plan and agrees to carry out the behavior specified.

5. The purposes of writing a contract are to specify what actions the individual will take in order to reach the goals set and to establish a means of evaluating this progress.

---

working out a contract. In their contracts they listed the behaviors to be monitored, noted their self-monitoring strategies, set forth rewards and punishers, and scheduled a maintenance review.

MAINTENANCE AND RELAPSE PREVENTION

Maintenance is one test of the usefulness of self-management training. The behavior change is likely to remain in effect if the individual has been allowed to practice the skills during the training program, is encouraged to practice these skills in different situations on the job, and continually self-monitors his or her performance of these new behaviors.

Maintenance strategies include training the employee to recognize common problems and pitfalls in applying self-management, as well as developing procedures for overcoming them. For the individual using self-management to reduce informal conversations, he or she should identify high-risk situations—such as going for coffee in the employee lounge or leaving the office door open—that are likely to cause the individual to be interrupted, stop self-managing and, consequently, not meet the desired goals. Once a number of these situations are identified, the individual can prevent relapse by learning to recognize and avoid these high-risk circumstances.

Another essential key to the individual's ability to maintain self-managing behaviors in the workplace lies in the environment in which the person is working. It is important that social reinforcement is provided when these self-management behaviors do occur. For example, if a manager is aware that an employee is trying to change

Figure 5.21
Contracts

A. Features of a Good Contract

  1. Specific statements of the techniques that you will use in specific situations.

  2. Goals and subgoals, which should be formulated precisely enough so that you can compare them to your performance and know exactly if you have achieved the goal.

  3. Feedback, which is information about your current level of performance provided by your self-monitoring and recording. Without some information about your performance, you can't correct yourself. You must continue to self-monitor and record so that self-correction can occur.

  4. Comparison of feedback and goals, which can result in some changes in the contract. In this step, you will record your self-observations and compare them to your goal.

B. Steps When Working Out a Contract

  1. State your goal(s). If it is a complex goal, or one that will take a long time to reach, state the goal(s) in terms of a short-term period.

  2. State your current level of performance.

  3. Use this information to set your subgoals.

  4. Be specific about your subgoals. State the situations and behaviors in which these goals will be performed.

  5. Be sure that you have accurate self-observation and feedback.

  6. Compare your performance to the goals you set.

Source: Adapted from *Self-Directed Behavior: Self-Modification for Personal Adjustment,* fourth edition, by D. L. Watson and R. G. Tharp. Copyright 1984 by Wadsworth, Inc. Reprinted by permission of the publisher, Brooks/Cole Publishing Company, Pacific Grove, California.

certain behaviors and sees an improvement in the employee's progress, acknowledging this improvement can have a positive impact on the employee and stimulate him or her to continue this behavior. Encouraging and reinforcing self-management in subordinates and managers alike can help develop and maintain an environment where self-management capabilities can be utilized effectively.

In Week 7, each individual was trained to recognize common problems and pitfalls in applying self-management techniques as well

Figure 5.22
Trainee's Contract
Effective dates: September 23, 1986 to December 12, 1986

The following behavior(s) will be monitored by me:

BEHAVIOR(S):

1. Attendance on the job (8 hours each day).
2. Absenteeism (# hours not present at the work site when I am scheduled to be there).
3. The number of interactions with my boss regarding my job performance on a specific project.
4. The behaviors I exhibit during the interaction.
5. The status of my asthma condition.

SELF-MONITORING:

1,2. I will record daily the number of hours I am on and off the job when I was scheduled to be there. In addition, when I don't come to work, I will record the reason(s) why directly under the specific date on the chart.

3. I will monitor my interactions with my supervisor when she reviews my work completed for that particular week. I will record both pleasant and unpleasant interactions with her and the situations/circumstances under which the interaction occurred.

4. I will monitor my thoughts and feelings prior to my decision to leave early, and the consequences that occur as a result of my decision. I will also pay close attention to the environment that we are in at the time and any other co-workers who might be there as well.

REWARDS/PUNISHERS:

1,2. Each week I have a perfect attendance record I will treat myself and my husband to an ice cream cone at Farfar's. After two consecutive weeks of perfect attendance, I will reduce the frequency of the reward to twice every month on Friday evenings. At the end of three months, I will no longer use this extrinsic reinforcer and will use positive oral reinforcement only. Each week I miss any hours not due to scheduled medical appointments or previous engagements, I will forfeit playing cards with my friends on Saturday evening.

3,4. I will not use any extrinsic reinforcers or punishers for either behavior listed in 3 and 4. Simply being able to get along with my supervisor

98

Figure 5.22 (continued)

without breaking down and leaving work early, or getting into an argument with my husband as a result of leaving early will be rewarding enough. If I don't succeed in meeting my goals, I consider that a strong punisher in itself.

MAINTENANCE:

This contract will be reviewed during the week of December 17th, 1986 by me and the trainer.

Signature(s): _____

(Trainee #4)

_____

(Program Trainer)

Figure 5.23
Contract Case Study

Fred Smith is now ready to write his contract. You have helped him identify what the problem behaviors are, learn how to set goals based on these behaviors, and learn how to reward or punish oneself for meeting or failing to meet self-set goals.

During this training session, you have learned that a good way of organizing the information regarding goals, rewards, and punishers as well as committing to the goals that you have set is to form a written plan or contract. Once again, placing yourself in Fred's role:

1. What would your contract for the self-management of attendance behavior look like?

2. List all the relevant information that should be included in the contract.

3. What type of checklist should you use to see if your plan looks like it will work?

4. What are the strengths of the contract? The weaknesses? How often will you examine your contract for possible changes? Deletions? Additions?

Figure 5.24
Maintenance Principles

---

1. Not every plan will work perfectly; there are sometimes unexpected problems or flaws that need to be worked out.
2. Three frequently encountered problems are:
   a) The individual stops self-monitoring.
   b) The program is not applied or not maintained over time.
   c) The program is applied, but there is no change in the target behavior. (Andrasik & Heimberg, 1982).
3. You need to assess your progress periodically. Self-management techniques may be applied at any time.

Figure 5.25
Techniques for Implementing Maintenance Strategies

---

1. If your target behavior is not responding to your change efforts, then you haven't identified what really rewards you.
2. You must use a variety of reward options to avoid satiation.
3. If you are now giving yourself continuous reinforcement for performing your target behavior, start "thinning out" the schedule.
4. As you work with your behavior, your sense of what you really want to strengthen may become more precise. This facilitates maintenance.
5. If relapse does occur, use it as a valuable opportunity to learn, rather than as a failure.
6. In planning for long-term maintenance, you should begin to explore and clarify the range of situations in which your behavior pays off for you.
7. The objective of using maintenance strategies is to have your target behavior become a permanent, strong part of your normal behavior.

as strategies for overcoming them (Andrasik & Heimberg, 1982). The training focused on preventing relapse by having the trainees identify high-risk situations for relapse, planning ahead for such situations, and utilizing coping strategies to deal with potentially problematic situations (Andrasik & Heimberg, 1982; Marx, 1982). Examples of principles of maintenance behavior discussed as well as techniques for implementing them are shown in Figures 5.24 and 5.25, respectively. Questions for identifying appropriate maintenance strategies (Figure 5.26) were provided during the session to aid

Figure 5.26
Maintenance Strategies

QUESTIONS TO IDENTIFY APPROPRIATE STRATEGIES:

1. How frequently will the pinpointed behavior be measured in the maintenance phase of your program?
2. Indicate any other changes in the way you measure the behavior.
3. Select one (or more) maintenance strategies listed below:
   a) Reduce frequency of pleasant consequence.
      Change frequency to _____.
   b) Reduce intensity of pleasant consequence.
      Change intensity by _____.
   c) Change form of consequence to conform with less frequent administration or reduce intensity.
      Change consequence to _____.

---

the trainees in generating ideas. Individuals were instructed to practice the techniques in a variety of situations and to continue to self-monitor attendance behavior after the training program ended. A questionnaire (Figure 3.6) was administered three months and again six months after the training to assess whether the trainees continued to use the skills taught in class.

The case study (Figure 5.27) gave the trainees an opportunity to work out maintenance and relapse prevention techniques. At this point, in addition, they were introduced to the troubleshooting worksheet concept (Figure 5.28): making a chart for recording problems and solutions as the self-management process continued. This worksheet was designed to aid the trainee in identifying areas that might be particularly troublesome and serve as an obstacle to effective self-managing.

ADVANTAGES OF SELF-MANAGEMENT

Extending beyond these two studies and the area of absenteeism, self-management has a number of additional advantages. First, management by self is less expensive than management by others. Second, since many individuals unknowingly engage in counterproductive self-management, knowledge of effective self-management strategies may enable them to improve their situations. Third, knowledge of self-management strategies enables the manager to instruct others in its use. Fourth, self-management can be inexpen-

Figure 5.27
Maintenance/Relapse Prevention Case Study

The last step in formulating a self-management plan is to build in ways to assure that the new behavior(s) will become a permanent part of your normal behavior patterns. Often, there are situations, people, and a combination of both that serve as potential obstacles to maintaining the target behavior.

Fred Smith needs to create ways of maintaining his attendance on the job—especially since he is once again being considered for promotion and we all know that last time he was denied this opportunity because of his poor on-the-job attendance and subsequent performance.

1. What steps would you suggest to help Fred maintain his attendance on the job?
2. What are some specific strategies that he can use to overcome potential relapse situations?
3. What are some of the telltale signs that could indicate a problem with maintaining his newly learned behavior(s)?
4. What should he do if he finds himself once again returning to old patterns of behavior?

sive relative to organizational reward systems. Fifth, and perhaps of most importance, the practice of self-management can be more congruent with organizational trends such as downsized operations, offices in the home, employee need for autonomy, and growth in the service sector.

While self-management has several advantages, there are some considerations that must be taken into account when choosing to use a self-management program. First, some individuals do not want to self-manage or be self-managed. They feel perhaps that they are already effectively managing themselves. Second, most studies have found that individuals should practice self-management techniques with one behavior at a time that they want to work on. In this way the person is able to make a single concerted effort by focusing on managing one behavior at a time. Third, the person must possess a strong commitment to change. Without a firm belief on the part of the individual that he or she wants to set and commit to the goals of self-managing, any efforts in that direction will be fruitless. Fourth, the individual must self-record and assess data in a systematic fashion. If the individual is not motivated to keep track and monitor

Figure 5.28
Troubleshooting Worksheet

The following chart can be used as an aid to assessing the problems you are having with the program and keeping a record of the solutions you used.

DATE   PROBLEM   ACTION TAKEN   RESULT

his or her own behavior, the self-management process will be short-lived at most. Fifth, and perhaps most important, the research in self-management is relatively untested. While the results presented in this book suggest powerful evidence for the results of practicing effective self-management, clearly more research and practice is warranted.

SUMMARY

Self-management training teaches the basic techniques and then measures trainees' performance over time. The specific strategies and procedures for developing self-management behavior in employees follow this sequence:

1. Self-assessment
2. Goal setting
3. Self-monitoring
4. Self-evaluation (self-reinforcement and self-punishment)
5. Contracts
6. Maintenance and relapse prevention

These steps are combined in an eight-week training program for achieving effective self-management skills. Overall advantages of self-management include cost, the ease with which managers can instruct their employees, and its appropriateness to new workplace situations of the future. The findings of these studies provide several directions for future research, epecially with regard to other workplace problem behaviors.

6

OTHER APPLICATIONS OF SELF-MANAGEMENT IN THE WORKPLACE

As indicated in Chapter 5, self-management training for increasing employee attendance is only one area in which self-management has proven effective. Other managerial applications of self-management—awaiting future research—include improving performance, managing the complexity of international assignments, and reducing stress in the workplace. Each of these applications is touched on below.

MANAGERIAL PERFORMANCE

As discussed earlier, employees' demands for flexibility, autonomy, and challenge are increasing. In an effort to deal with these increased demands, managers are struggling to find an approach that accommodates both the employees' need for freedom and the organization's need for control and effective performance. Self-management training may provide an effective solution.

Several case studies (Luthans & Davis, 1979) have shown the success of self-management training for improving performance

among managers in a variety of fields—retailing, advertising, manufacturing, and public service. A wide range of behaviors, including
spending time on the phone, leaving one's own work to assist others,
failure to get to work on time, writing a plan, following the plan, and
dealing with subordinates' deviations from the plan, were identified
by these managers as behaviors they wanted to improve upon in
order to increase their effectiveness on the job. With systematic
application of self-management, the managers did improve these
behaviors and increase their effectiveness.

Manz and Sims (1980) described self-management as a "substitute
for leadership" (Kerr & Jermier, 1977) in that it teaches a subordinate to exercise control over the same contingencies of reinforcement
available to the subordinate's supervisor. Implicit in this view is that
employee self-management can be instrumental in furthering organizational goals by freeing supervisors to perform other important
tasks (e.g., strategic planning). Manz and Sims' (1980) work has
involved the use of self-managed work groups in industrial settings,
the use of self-management training for entrepreneurs, and development of self-leadership capabilities in subordinates.

In the face of competing demands on time and resources, it is
essential that a manager have clearly stated objectives. But objectives
alone are not sufficient for managing effectively within an often
unpredictable and chaotic work environment. Training in self-
management can improve an individual's behavior and lead to the
exercise of greater control over aspects of his or her decision making
and performance. Further empirical work is needed in this area to
examine the effectiveness of this training for employee performance
in organizational settings.

MANAGING INTERNATIONAL JOINT VENTURE (IJV) ASSIGNMENTS

Joint ventures have become an important element of many firms'
international strategies. These ventures involve two or more legally
distinct organizations (the parents), each of which actively partici-
pates in the decision-making activities of the jointly owned entity.

IJVs represent a relatively small yet rapidly growing component of
world economic activity (Harrigan, 1985). IJVs also represent an
effective means for firms to cope with competitive and technological
challenges.

Yet despite their increased popularity and strategic importance,
IJVs have frequently failed to achieve their parent firms' objectives.

Many of the IJV performance problems have been linked to the complex managerial situations that these ventures lead to. The complexity arises from the coordination of two or more parent organizations—who may well be competitors—as well as problems in communication both with one another and with the jointly owned company.

The overall costs can be quite substantial. In addition to consuming large amounts of management time, money, and other scarce resources, an IJV may also expose critical aspects of a parent firm's strategy, technology, or other know-how to third-party firms, placing at risk the parent's long-term competitive position.

The IJV general manager is responsible for maintaining relationships with each of the parents as well as for running the venture. This job is often challenging, because the IJV general manager must respond to all of the parents' objectives, goals, and cultures as well as to geographic distances. This situation readily lends itself to self-management strategies to help the IJV general managers and other key employees gain control over such unpredictable environments. Frayne and Geringer (1990) have suggested a simple, 12-hour self-management training program for these individuals as one means of improving the management and performance of IJVs. Such a program could enhance an individual's self-efficacy within an IJV task environment, with its attendant high uncertainty and conflicting parent objectives.

REDUCING STRESS IN THE WORKPLACE

It was not until the early 1970s that a small group of researchers began studying the impact of work-related stress. Since that time a widespread concern with the effects of stress has developed.

Depression, anxiety, irritation, and anger are common results of work-related stress. These usually lead to job boredom, burnout, and/or withdrawal in the forms of absenteeism and turnover.

Stress has serious consequences for the organization as well—absenteeism, poor employee-management relations, poor productivity, high accident rates, high turnover, poor organizational climate, antagonism at work, job dissatisfaction, and decreased ability to make decisions (Cox, 1979).

As noted earlier, self-management has been effective in clinical psychology with such behaviors as weight control, drug addiction, alcohol abuse, and anxiety reduction. These behaviors are often caused by or are a direct result of an individual's stress or reaction to an inability to manage stress.

Research is needed on the direct application of self-management techniques to the reduction of employee stress. Clearly, focusing people's efforts on their most important goals must serve to minimize stress-inducing problems. So does helping them gain autonomy on the job. The successful empirical results in clinical psychology as well as the importance of this problem lend support to this avenue of research.

THE TIME IS NOW

Effective self-management offers many potential benefits to individual employees and organizations. From a cost-benefit perspective, self-management may represent an attractive route because it involves less expense in terms of dollars and time than traditional hierarchy-based techniques. It may also be much more effective than these in generating the desired behavior. Further, because all individuals appear to use some approach—either systematic or ad hoc—to manage their behaviors, the varying effectiveness of these individual methods is too important an issue for organizations to ignore. Indeed, many individuals engage in dysfunctional self-management. For example, a person who sets unrealistically high goals may become frustrated rather than motivated to achieve them. Systematic self-management should provide individuals with the time to engage in foresightful planning in addition to having positive effects on daily performance. Finally, the manager who is well versed in effective self-management can serve as a role model for his or her own subordinates in aiding them to develop more effective self-managing capabilities of their own.

It is only recently that researchers and practitioners have begun to realize the benefits to be derived from teaching self-management. Nevertheless, enormous amounts of time, money, and resources are still being spent training people in the "right" way to manage other people. Perhaps the time has come to train people how to manage themselves.

BIBLIOGRAPHY

Andrasik, F., and Heimberg, J. (1982). Self-management procedures. In L. W. Frederiksen (ed.), *Handbook of organizational behavior management* (pp. 219-248). New York: Wiley.

Arvey, R. D., Cole, D. A., Hazucha, J. F., and Hartanto, F. M. (1985). Statistical power of training evaluation designs. *Journal of Applied Psychology,* 38, 493-501.

As, D. (1962). Absenteeism: A social fact in need of a theory. *Acta Sociologica,* 6, 278-285.

Azrin, N. H. (1977). A strategy for applied research: Learning based but outcome oriented. *American Psychologist,* 32, 140-149.

Bandura, A. (1977a). Self-efficacy: Toward a unifying theory of behavior change. *Psychological Review,* 84, 191-215.

_____. (1977b). *Social learning theory.* Englewood Cliffs, NJ: Prentice-Hall.

_____. (1978a). Reflections on self-efficacy. *Advances in Behavior Research and Therapy,* 1, 237-269.

_____. (1978b). The self system in reciprocal determinism. *American Psy-*

chologist, 33, 344-358.

———. (1982). Self-efficacy mechanism in human agency. *American Psy-chologist,* 37, 122-147.

———. (1984). Recycling misconceptions of perceived self-efficacy. *Cognitive Therapy and Research,* 8, 231-255.

———. (1986). *Social foundations of thought and action: A social cognitive theory.* Englewood Cliffs, NY: Prentice-Hall.

Bandura, A., and Adams, N. E. (1977). Analysis of self-efficacy theory of behavioral change. *Cognitive Therapy and Research,* 1, 287-308.

Bandura, A., Adams, N. E., and Beyer, J. (1977). Cognitive processes mediating behavioral change. *Journal of Personality and Social Psychology,* 35, 125-139.

Bandura, A., Adams, N. E., Hardy, A. B., and Howells, G. N. (1980). Tests of the generality of self-efficacy theory. *Cognitive Therapy and Research,* 4, 39-66.

Bandura, A., and Barab, P. G. (1971). Conditions governing nonreinforcement imitation. *Developmental Psychology,* 5, 244-255.

Bandura, A., and Cervone, D. (1983). Self-evaluative and self-efficacy mechanisms governing the motivational effects of goal systems. *Journal of Personality and Social Psychology,* 45, 1017-1028.

Bandura, A., Reese, L., and Adams, N. E. (1982). Microanalysis of action and fear arousal as a function of differential levels of perceived self-efficacy. *Journal of Personality and Social Psychology,* 43, 5-21.

Bandura, A., and Simon, K. M. (1977). The role of proximal intentions in self-regulation of refractory behavior. *Cognitive Therapy and Research,* 1, 177-193.

Barling, J., and Abel, M. (1983). Self-efficacy beliefs and tennis performance. *Cognitive Therapy and Research,* 7, 265-272.

Barling, J., and Beattie, R. (1983). Self-efficacy beliefs and sales performance. *Journal of Organizational Behavior Management,* 5, 41-51.

Beneke, W. N., and Harris, M. B. (1972). Teaching self control of study behavior. *Behavior Therapy and Research,* 10, 35-41.

Bolles, R. C. (1972). Reinforcement, expectancy, and learning. *Psychological Review,* 79, 394-409.

Brief, A., and Aldag, R. (1981). The "self" in work organizations: A conceptual review. *Academy of Management Review,* 6, 75-88.

Bromley, D. G., and Shupe, A. D. (1979). *"Moonies" in America: Cult, church, crusade.* Beverly Hills: Sage.

Brownell, K., Marlatt, G., Lichtenstein, E., and Wilson, G. (1986). Relapse Prevention. *American Psychologist,* 41, 765-782.

Burnaska, R. F. (1976). The effects of behavior modeling training upon managers' behaviors and employees' perceptions. *Personnel Psychology,* 29, 329-335.

Byham, W. C., Adams, D., and Kiggins, A. (1976). Transfer of modeling training to the job. *Personnel Psychology,* 29, 345-349.

Campbell, D. T., and Stanley, J. C. (1980). *Experimental and quasi-experimental designs for research.* Chicago: Rand McNally.

Campbell, J. P. (1982). I/O psychology and the enhancement of productivity. Paper presented at the annual meeting of the American Psychological Association, Washington, D.C.

Chadwick-Jones, J. K., Brown, C. A., Nicholson, N., and Shephard, C. (1971). Absence measures: Their reliability and stability in an industrial setting. *Personnel Psychology,* 24, 463-470.

Chadwick-Jones, J. K., Nicholson, N., and Brown, C. A. (1982). *Social psychology of absenteeism.* New York: Praeger.

Clegg, C. W. (1983). Psychology of employee lateness, absence, and turnover: A methodological critique and an empirical study. *Journal of Applied Psychology,* 68, 88-101.

Cohen, J. (1977). *Statistical power analysis for the behavioral sciences.* New York: Academic.

Cook, T. D., and Campbell, D. T. (1979). *Quasi-experimental: Design and analysis issues for field setting.* Boston: Houghton Mifflin.

Coppel, D. (1982). The relationship of perceived social support and self-efficacy to major and minor stresses. Unpublished doctoral dissertation, University of Washington.

Cox, D. J. (1979). Differential effectiveness of electromyograph feedback, verbal relaxation instructions, and medication placebo with tension headaches. *Journal of Consulting and Clinical Psychology,* 43, 892-899.

Cruikshank, G. E. (1976). No shows at work: High-priced headache. *Nation's Business,* 37-39.

Cummings, L. L. (1981). Organizational behavior in the 1980's. *Decision Sciences,* 12, 365-377.

Davis, T., and Luthans, F. (1980). A social learning approach of organizational behavior. *Academy of Management Review,* 5, 281-290.

Davis, F. W., and Yates, B. T. (1982). Self-efficacy expectations versus outcome expectancies. *Cognitive Therapy and Research,* 6, 23-26.

DiClemente, C. C. (1981). Self-efficacy and smoking cessation maintenance: A preliminary report. *Cognitive Therapy and Research,* 5, 175-187.

Dulany, D. E. (1968). Awareness, rules and propositional control: A confrontation with s-r behavior theory. In T. R. Dixon and D. L. Horton (eds.), *Verbal behavior and general behavior therapy* (pp. 340-387). Englewood Cliffs, NJ: Prentice-Hall.

Dunnette, M. (1976). Mishmash, mush, and milestones in organizational psychology: 1974. In H. Meltzer and F. R. Wickert (eds.), *Humanizing organizational behavior.* Springfield, IL: Thomas.

Eastman, C., and Marzillier, J. S. (1984). Theoretical and methodological difficulties in Bandura's self-efficacy theory. *Cognitive Research and Therapy,* 8, 213-229.

Epstein, L. H., and Wing, R. R. (1979). Behavioral contracting: Health behaviors. *Clinical Behavior Therapy Review*, 1, 2-21.

Erez, M. (1977). Feedback: A necessary condition for the goal setting-performance relationship. *Journal of Applied Psychology*, 62, 69-78.

Erez, M., and Kanfer, F. H. (1983). The role of goal acceptance in goal setting and task performance. *Academy of Management Review*, 8, 454-463.

Feeney, E. J. (1973). *Behavioral engineering systems training*. Redding, CT: Feeney.

Feltz, D. (1982). Path analysis of the causal elements in Bandura's theory of self-efficacy and an anxiety-based model of avoidance behavior. *Journal of Personality and Social Psychology*, 42, 764-781.

Fichman, M. (1984). A theoretical approach to understanding absence. In P. Goodman and R. Atkin (eds.), *Absenteeism: New approaches to understanding, measuring, and managing employee absence* (pp. 1-46). San Francisco: Jossey-Bass.

Ford, J. E. (1981). A simple punishment procedure for controlling employee absenteeism. *Journal of Organizational Behavior Management*, 3, 71-79.

Frayne, C. A. (1986). The application of social learning theory to employee self-management of attendance. Unpublished doctoral dissertation, University of Washington.

Frayne, C. A., and Geringer, J. M. (forthcoming). The strategic use of human resource management techniques as control mechanisms in international joint ventures. In K. Rowland and G. Ferris (eds.), *Research in Personnel & Human Resource Management*. JAI Press.

Frayne, C. A., and Latham, G. P. (1987). The application of social learning theory to employee self-management of attendance. *Journal of Applied Psychology*, 72, 387-392.

Georgopoulous, B. S., Mahoney, G. M., and Jones, W. (1957). A path-goal approach to productivity. *Journal of Applied Psychology*, 41, 345-353.

Glasgow, R. E., Klesges, R. C., Godding, P. R., and Gegelman, P. (1983). Controlled smoking, with or without carbon monoxide feedback as an alternative for chronic smokers. *Behavior Therapy*, 14, 386-397.

Glynn, E. L. (1970). Classroom applications of self-determined reinforcement. *Journal of Applied Behavior Analysis*, 3, 123-132.

Godding, P. R., and Glasgow, R. E. (1985). Self-efficacy and outcome expectations as predictors of controlled smoking status. *Cognitive Therapy and Research*, 9, 583-590.

Goldstein, A. P., and Kanfer, F. H. (1979). *Maximizing treatment gains*. New York: American.

Goldstein, A. P., and Sorcher, M. (1974). *Changing supervisory behavior*. New York: Pergamon.

Goldstein, I. L. (1980). Training in work organizations. *Annual Review of Psychology* (vol. 31, pp. 229-272). Palo Alto, CA: Annual Reviews.

Goodman, P. S. (1979). *Assessing organizational change: The Rushton quality of work experiment.* New York: Wiley Interscience.

Goodman, P. S., and Atkin, R. S. (1984). Effects of absenteeism on individuals and organizations. In P. S. Goodman and R. S. Atkin (eds.), *Absenteeism: New approaches to understanding, measuring, and managing employee absence* (pp. 276-321). San Francisco: Jossey-Bass.

Greenwald, A. G. (1980). The totalitarian ego: Fabrication and revision of personal history. *American Psychologist,* 35, 603-618.

Hall, S. M. (1980). Self-management and therapeutic maintenance: Theory and research. In P. Karoly and J. J. Steffen (eds.), *Improving the long-term effects of psychotherapy: Models of durable outcome.* New York: Garden-Press.

Hamner, T. H., Landau, J. C., and Stern, R. N. (1981). Absenteeism when workers have a voice: The case of employee ownership. *Journal of Applied Psychology,* 66, 561-573.

Hamner, T. H., and Landau, J. C. (1981). Methodological issues in the use of absence data. *Journal of Applied Psychology,* 66, 574-581.

Harrigan, K. R. (1985). *Strategies for Joint Ventures.* Lexington, Mass: Lexington Books, 1985.

Hays, W. L. (1973). *Statistics for the social sciences.* 2nd ed. New York: Holt, Rinehart and Winston.

Hedges, J. N. (1973). Absence from work—a look at some national data. *Monthly Labor Review* (July), 24-30.

Heyduk, R. G., and Fenigstein, A. (1984). Influential works and authors in psychology: A survey of eminent psychologists. *American Psychologist,* 39, 556-559.

Hinrichs, J. R. (1978). *Practical management of productivity.* New York: Van Nostrand Reinhold.

Hulin, C. (1984). Suggested directions for defining, measuring, and controlling absenteeism. In P. S. Goodman and R. S. Atkin (eds.), *Absenteeism: New approaches to understanding, measuring, and managing employee absence* (pp. 391-420). San Francisco: Jossey-Bass.

Hull, C. L., (1943). *Principles of behavior.* New York: Appleton-Century-Crofts.

Ilgen, D. (1977). Attendance behavior: a reevaluation of Latham & Pursell's conclusions. *Journal of Applied Psychology,* 62, 230-233.

Johns, G. (1984). Unresolved issues in the study and management of absence from work. In P. S. Goodman and R. S. Atkin (eds.), *Absenteeism: New approaches to understanding, measuring, and managing employee absence* (pp. 360-390). San Francisco: Jossey-Bass.

Johns, G., and Nicholson, N. (1982). The meanings of absence: New strategies for theory and research. In B. M. Staw and L. L. Cummings (eds.), *Research in organizational behavior* (vol. 1, pp. 127-172). Greenwich, CT: JAI.

Kanfer, F. H. (1970). Self-regulation : Research, issues, and speculations. In C. Neuringer and J. L. Michael (eds.), *Behavior modification in clinical psychology* (pp. 178-220). New York: Appleton-Century-Crofts.

_____. (1975). Self-management methods. In F. H. Kanfer and A. P. Goldstein (eds.), *Helping people change* (pp. 309-355). New York: Pergamon.

_____. (1980). Self-management methods. In F. H. Kanfer and A. P. Goldstein (eds.), *Helping people change: A textbook of methods.* 2nd ed. (pp. 309-355). New York: Pergamon.

_____. (1986). Implications of a self-regulation model of therapy for treatment of addictive behaviors. In W. R. Miller and N. Heather (eds.), *Treating addictive behaviors. Vol. II., Processes of change* (pp. 272-314). New York: Plenum.

Kanfer, F. H., and Bursemeyer, J. R., (1982). The use of problem solving and decision making in behavior therapy. *Clinical Psychology Review,* 2, 239-266.

Kanfer, F. H., Cox, L. E., Greiner, J. M., and Karoly, P. (1974). Contracts, demand characteristics, and self-control. *Journal of Personality and Social Psychology,* 30, 605-619.

Kanfer, F. H., and Karoly, P. (1972). Self-control : A behavioristic excursion into the lion's den. *Behavior Therapy,* 3, 398-416.

Kanfer, F. H., and Phillips, J. (1970). *Learning foundations of behavior therapy.* New York: Wiley.

Karoly, P., and Kanfer, F. H. (1982). *Self-management and behavior change: From theory to practice.* New York: Pergamon.

Kaufman, A., Baron, A., and Kopp, R. E. (1966). Some effects of instructions on human operant behavior. *Psychonomic Monograph Supplements,* 1, 243-250.

Kazdin, A. E. (1978). Conceptual and assessment issues raised by self-efficacy theory. *Advances in Behavior Research and Therapy,* 1, 177-185.

Kazdin, A. E., and Wilson, G. T. (1978). *Evaluation of behavior therapy: Issues, evidence, and research strategies.* Cambridge, MA: Ballinger.

Kendall, G. P., and Stuart, A. (1958). *The advanced theory of statistics.* New York: Hafner.

Kerr, S., and Jermier, J. (1977). Substitutes for leadership: Their meaning and measurement. *Organizational Behavior and Human Performance,* 22, 375-403.

Kirkpatrick, D. L. (1967). Evaluation of training. In R. L. Craig (ed.),

Training and development handbook: A guide to human resource development (pp. 337-352). New York: McGraw-Hill.

Komaki, J., Waddell, W. M., and Pearce, M. G. (1977). The applied behavior analysis approach and individual employees: Improving performance in two small businesses. *Organizational Behavior and Human Performance,* 19, 337-352.

Korman, A. (1970). Toward a hypothesis of work behavior. *Journal of Applied Psychology,* 54, 31-41.

———. (1976). Hypothesis of work behavior revisited and an extension. *Academy of Management Review,* 1, 50-63.

Kraut, A. J. (1976). Behavior modeling symposium: Developing managerial skills via modeling techniques. *Personnel Psychology,* 29, 325-328.

Latham, G. P., and Frayne, C. A. (1986). The stability of job attendance. Unpublished manuscript, University of Washington.

Latham, G. P., and Frayne, C. A. (1989). Self-management training for increasing employee attendance: A follow-up and a replication. *Journal of Applied Psychology,* 74.

Latham, G. P., and Lee, T. (1986). Goal setting. In E. A. Locke (ed.), *Generalizing from laboratory to field settings* (pp. 101-118). Boston: D.C. Heath.

Latham, G. P., Mitchell, T. R., and Dossett, D. L. (1978). The importance of participative goal setting and anticipated rewards on goal difficulty and job performance. *Journal of Applied Psychology,* 63, 173-181.

Latham, G. P., and Napier, N. K. (1984). Practical ways to increase employee attendance. In P. S. Goodman and R. S. Atkin (eds.), *Absenteeism: New approaches to understanding, measuring, and managing employee absence* (pp. 322-359). San Francisco: Jossey-Bass.

Latham, G. P., and Pursell, E. D. (1975). Measuring absenteeism from the opposite side of the coin. *Journal of Applied Psychology,* 60, 369-371.

———. (1977). Measuring attendance: A reply to Ilgen. *Journal of Applied Psychology,* 62, 239-246.

Latham, G. P., and Saari, L. M. (1979). The application of social learning theory to training supervisors through behavioral modeling. *Journal of Applied Psychology,* 64, 635-642.

Latham, G. P., Saari, L. M., Pursell, E. D., and Campion, M. A. (1980). The situational interview. *Journal of Applied Psychology,* 65, 422-427.

Latham, G. P., and Saari, L. M. (1984). Do people do what they say? Further studies on the situational interview. *Journal of Applied Psychology,* 69, 569-573.

Latham, G. P., and Yukl, G. A. (1975). A review of research on the application of goal setting in organizations. *Academy of Management Review,* 18, 824-845.

Lee, C. (1982). Self-efficacy as a predictor of performance in competitive gymnastics. *Journal of Sports Psychology,* 4, 405-409.

_____. (1984a). Accuracy of efficacy and outcome expectations in predicting performance in a simulated assertiveness task. *Cognitive Therapy and Research,* 8, 37-48.

_____. (1984b). Efficacy expectations and outcome expectations as predictors of performance in a snake-handling task. *Cognitive Therapy and Research,* 8, 509-516.

_____. (1985). Efficacy expectations as predictors of performance: Meaningful measures of microanalytic match. *Cognitive Therapy and Research,* 9, 367-370.

Lewin, K. (1938). The conceptual representation and the measurement of psychological forces. *Contributions to psychological theory.* Durham, NC: Duke University Press, 1, no. 4.

_____. (1947). Frontiers in group dynamics. *Human Relations,* 1, 5-41.

Lichenstein, E., and Condiotte, M. (1981). Self-efficacy and relapse in smoking cessation programs. *Journal of Consulting and Clinical Psychology,* 49, 648-658.

Locke, E. A. (1968). Toward a theory of task motivation and incentives. *Organizational Behavior and Human Performance,* 3, 157-189.

_____. (1975). Personal attitudes and motivation. *Annual Review of Psychology,* 26, 457-480.

_____. (1977). The myths of behavior mod in organizations. *Academy of Management Review,* 4, 131-136.

Locke, E. A., Frederick, E., Lee, C., and Bobko, P. (1984). Effect of self-efficacy, goals, and task strategies on task performance. *Journal of Applied Psychology,* 69, 241-253.

Locke, E., and Latham, G. P. (1984). *Goal setting: A motivational technique that works!* Englewood Cliffs, NJ: Prentice-Hall.

Locke, E. A., Shaw, K., Saari, L. M., and Latham, G. P. (1981). Goal setting and task performance: 1969-1980. *Psychological Bulletin,* 90, 125-152.

Luthans, F., and Davis, T. R. V. (1979). Behavioral self-management: The missing link in managerial effectiveness. *Organizational Dynamics,* 8, 42-60.

Maddux, J. E., Sherer, M., and Rogers, R. W. (1982). Self-efficacy expectancy: Their relationship and their effects. *Cognitive Therapy and Research,* 6, 207-212.

Mahoney, M. J., Moura, N. G., and Wade, T. C. (1973). The relative efficacy of self-reward, self-punishment, and self-monitoring techniques for weight loss. *Journal of Consulting and Clinical Psychology,* 40, 404-407.

Manning, M. M., and Wright, T. L. (1983). Self-efficacy expectations, outcome expectations, and the persistence of pain in childbirth. *Journal of Personality and Social Psychology,* 45, 421-431.

Manz, C. C. (1983). *The art of self-leadership.* Englewood Cliffs, NJ: Prentice-Hall.

Manz, C., and Sims, H. P., Jr. (1980). Self-management as a substitute for leadership. *Academy of Management Review,* 5, 361-367.

Mardia, K. (1971). The effect of nonnormality on some multivariate tests and robustness of nonnormality in the linear model. *Biometrika,* 58, 105-121.

Marlatt, G., and Gordon, J. (eds.). *Relapse prevention: Maintenance strategies in addictive behavior change.* New York: Guilford.

Marx, R. (1982). Relapse prevention for managerial training: A model for maintenance of behavior change. *Academy of Management Review,* 7, 433-441.

McGhee, W., and Tuller, W. I. (1978). A note on evaluating behavior modification and behavior modeling as industrial training techniques. *Personnel Psychology,* 31, 477-484.

Mills, P. M. (1983). Self-management: Its control and relationship to other organizational properties. *Academy of Management Review,* 8, 445-453.

Mitchell, T. R. (1974). Expectancy models of job satisfaction, occupational preference, and effort: A theoretical, methodological, and empirical appraisal. *Psychological Bulletin,* 81, 1053-1077.

————. (1979). Organizational behavior. *Annual Review of Psychology,* 30, 243-281.

————. (1982). Motivation: New directions for theory, research and practice. *Academy of Management Review,* 7, 80-88.

Moses, J. L., and Ritchie, R. J. (1976). Supervisory relationships training: A behavioral evaluation of a behavior modeling program. *Personnel Psychology,* 29, 337-343.

Mowday, R. T., Porter, L. W., and Steers, R. M. (1982). *Employee-organization linkages: The psychology of commitment, absenteeism, and turnover.* New York: Academic.

Muchinsky, P. (1977). Employee absenteeism: A review of the literature. *Journal of Vocational Behavior,* 10, 316-340.

Neter, J., and Wasserman, W. (1974). *Applied linear statistical models.* Homewood, IL: Irwin.

Nicholson, N. (1976). Management sanctions and absence control. *Human Relations,* 29, 139-151.

Nicholson, N., and Johns, G. (1982). The absence culture and the psychological contract—Who's in control of absence? Paper presented at the 20th International Congress of Applied Psychology, Edinburgh, Scotland, August.

_____. (1985). The absence culture and the psychological contract—Who's in control of absence? *Academy of Management Review,* 10, 397-407.

Nord, W. R. (1969). Beyond the teaching machine: The neglected area of operant conditioning in the theory and practice of management. *Organizational Behavior and Human Performance,* 4, 375-401.

O'Banion, D. R., and Whaley, D. L. (1981). *Behavioral contracting: Arranging contingencies of reinforcement.* New York: Springer.

Olds, J. (1958). Self-stimulation of the brain. *Science,* 127, 315-323.

Olds, J., and Milner, P. (1954). Positive reinforcement produced by electrical stimulation of septal area and other regions of a rat's brain. *Journal of Comparative Physiological Psychology,* 47, 419-427.

Pentz, M. A., and Kazdin, A. E. (1982). Assertion modeling stimuli effects on assertive behavior and self-efficacy in adolescents. *Behavior Research and Therapy,* 20, 365-371.

Richards, C. S. (1976). When self-control fails: Selective bibliography of research on the maintenance problems in self-control treatment programs. *JSAS Catalog of Selected Documents in Psychology,* 8, 67-68.

Rosenthal, R., and Zimmerman, B. J. (1978). *Social learning and cognition.* New York: Academic.

Rosenthal, T. L. (1978). Bandura's self-efficacy theory: Thought is father to the deed. *Advances in Behavior Research and Therapy,* 1, 203-209.

Ross, L. (1977). The intuitive psychologist and his shortcomings: Distortions in the attribution process. In L. Berkowitz (ed.), *Advances in experimental social psychology* (vol. 10, pp. 174-220). New York: Academic.

Rosse, J. G., and Miller, H. E. (1984). Relationship between absenteeism and other employee behaviors. In P. S. Goodman and R. S. Atkin (eds.), *Absenteeism: New approaches to understanding, measuring, and managing employee absence* (pp. 194-228). San Francisco: Jossey-Bass.

Rotter, J. B. (1966). Generalized expectancies for internal versus external control of reinforcement. *Psychological Monographs,* 80 (1, whole no. 609).

Ryan, T. A. (1970). *Intentional behavior.* New York: Ronald.

Saari, L. M., and Latham, G. P. (1982). Employee reactions to continuous and variable ration reinforcement schedules involving a monetary incentive. *Journal of Applied Psychology,* 67, 506-508.

Schmidt, F. L. (1973). Implications of a measurement problem for expectancy theory. *Organization Behavior and Human Performance,* 10, 243-251.

Skinner, B. F. (1953). *Science and human behavior.* New York: Macmillan.

Simon, K. N. (1979). Self-evaluative reactions: The role of personal valuation of the activity. *Cognitive Therapy and Research,* 3, 111-116.

Slocum, J., and Sims, H. (1980). A typology for integrating technology, organization, and job design. *Human Relations,* 33, 193-212.

Smith, P. E. (1976). Management modeling training to improve morale and customer satisfaction. *Personnel Psychology,* 29, 351-359.

Smulders, P. G. (1980). Comments on employee absence/attendance as a dependent variable in organizational research. *Journal of Applied Psychology,* 65, 368-371.

Snyder, M. (1980). Seek, and ye shall find: Testing hypotheses about other people. In E. T. Higgins, C. P. Herman, and M. P. Zanna (eds.), *Social cognition: The Ontario symposium on personality and social psychology* (vol. 1, pp. 105-130). Hillsdale, NJ: Erlbaum.

Staw, B. (1977). Motivation in organizations: Toward synthesis and redirection. In B. M. Staw and G. R. Salancik (eds.), *New directions in organizational behavior* (pp. 105-130). Chicago: St. Clair.

Steers, R. M., and Porter, L. W. (1974). The role of task-goal attributes in employee performance. *Psychological Bulletin,* 81, 434-452.

Steers, R. M., and Rhodes, S. R. (1978). Major influences on employee attendance: A process model. *Journal of Applied Psychology,* 63, 391-407.

_____. (1980). A new look at absenteeism. *Personnel* (Nov.-Dec.), 60-65.

_____. (1984). Knowledge and speculation about absenteeism. In P. S. Goodman and R. S. Atkin (eds.), *Absenteeism: New approaches to understanding, measuring, and managing employee absence* (pp. 229-275). San Francisco: Jossey-Bass.

Taylor, M. S., Locke, E. A., Lee, C., and Gist, M. E. (1984). Type A behavior and faculty research productivity: What are the mechanisms? *Organizational Behavior and Human Performance,* 34, 402-418.

Terborg, J., Lee, T. W., Smith, J. F., Davis, A. G., and Turbin, S. M. (1982). Extension of the Schmidt and Hunter validity generalization procedure to the prediction of absenteeism behavior from knowledge of job satisfaction and organizational commitment. *Journal of Applied Psychology,* 67, 440-449.

Thoresen, C. E., and Mahoney, M. J. (1974). *Behavioral self-control.* New York: Holt, Rinehart, and Winston.

Thorndike, E. L. (1911). Animal intelligence: An experimental study of the associative processes in animals. *Psychological Review Monographs Supplement,* 2, 1-9.

Thorndike, R. L., (1949). *Personnel selection.* New York: Wiley.

Thorpe, J. G., Schmidt, E., and Castell, D. A. (1963). A version-relief therapy: A new method for general application. *Behavior Research and Therapy,* 2, 71-82.

Tolman, E. C. (1932). *Purposive behavior in animals and men.* New York: Century.

Vroom, V. (1964). *Work and motivation.* New York: Wiley.

Watson, C. J., Driver, R. W., and Watson, K. D. (1985). Methodological issues in absenteeism research: Multiple absence measures and multivariate normality. *Academy of Management Review,* 10, 577-586.

Watson, D. L., and Tharp, R. G. (1981). *Self-directed behavior: Self-modification for personal adjustment.* 2nd ed. Monterey, CA: Brooks/Cole.

_____. (1984). *Self-directed behavior: Self-modification for personal adjustment.* 3rd ed. Monterey, CA: Brooks/Cole.

Wexley, K. N. (1984). Personnel training. *Annual Review of Psychology,* 35, 519-551.

Wexley, K. N., and Latham, G. P. (1981). *Developing and training human resources in organizations.* Glenview, IL: Scott Foresman.

Winer, B. J. (1971). *Statistical principles in experimental design.* 2nd ed. New York: McGraw-Hill.

Wolpin, J., and Burke, R. J. (1985). Relationships between absenteeism and turnover: A function of the measures? *Personnel Psychology,* 38, 57-74.

Yolles, J., Carone, A., and Krinske, E. (1975). *Absenteeism in industry.* Springfield, IL: Thomas.

INDEX

Absenteeism, 2-3, 16; and behavior, 20; motivation and ability, 19-20; research studies on, 45, 47-48, 58-63; social or cultural view of, 20; study on effects of self-management training on, 26-50; variables affecting, 19; withdrawal theory on, 20

Absenteeism measurement: absence versus presence of behavior, 21; attendance as dependent variable, 21-22; frequency and time lost, 21; multivariate analyses in, 22-23; non-normal sample distributions, 22; Type II error in, 23

Analysis of variance (ANOVA), 56, 64

AT&T, behavior modeling at, 14

Behavioral theories: drive theory in, 8, 9; operant conditioning in, 8, 9-10

Behavior modeling, 7, 13-14; differences with self-management 14-15

Cognitive theories: expectancy theory in, 11-12; goal-setting theory in, 12

Drive increased theory (Olds and Milner), 9

Drive reduction theory (Hull), 8, 9

Efficacy. *See* Self-efficacy

Emery Air Freight, study on reinforcement theory, 9

About the Author

COLETTE A. FRAYNE is Assistant Professor of Management in the School of Business Administration at the University of Western Ontario. She has been the recipient of numerous awards including the Academy of Management Best Paper Based on a Dissertation and the S. Rains Wallace Dissertation Award from the American Psychological Association.